# THE MUSCULAR SYSTEM

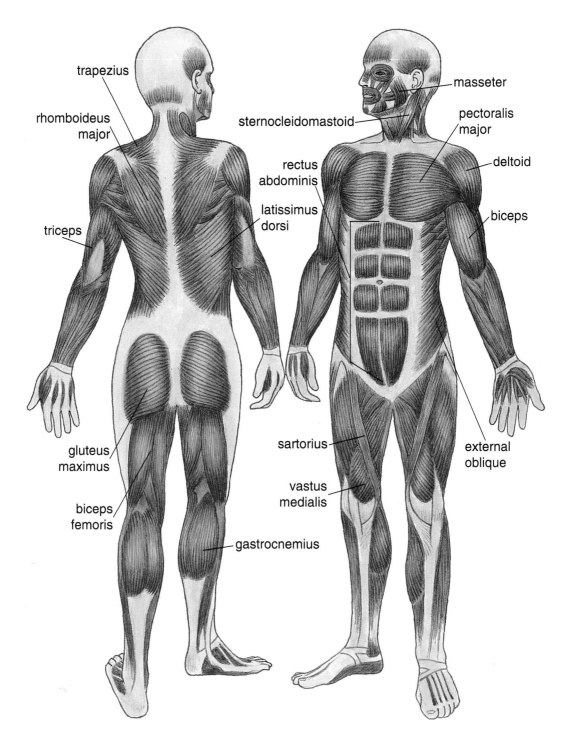

trapezius

rhomboideus
major

triceps

gluteus
maximus

biceps
femoris

gastrocnemius

masseter

sternocleidomastoid

rectus
abdominis

latissimus
dorsi

pectoralis
major

deltoid

biceps

sartorius

vastus
medialis

external
oblique

*The Muscular System*

**HUMAN BODY SYSTEMS**

# THE
# MUSCULAR
# SYSTEM

## Dr. Alvin, Virginia, and Robert Silverstein

**TWENTY-FIRST CENTURY BOOKS**
A Division of Henry Holt and Company
New York

Twenty-First Century Books
A Division of Henry Holt and Company, Inc.
115 West 18th Street
New York, NY 10011

Henry Holt ® and colophon are trademarks of
Henry Holt and Company, Inc.
*Publishers since 1866*

Published in Canada by Fitzhenry & Whiteside Ltd.
195 Allstate Parkway, Markham, Ontario L3R 4T8

**Library of Congress Cataloging-in-Publication Data**
Silverstein, Alvin.
Muscular system / Alvin, Virginia, and Robert Silverstein.—1st ed.
p.   cm. — (Human body systems)
Includes index.
1. Muscles—Juvenile literature. 2. Muscles—Diseases—Juvenile literature. [1. Muscles. 2. Muscular
system.] I. Silverstein, Virginia B. II. Silverstein, Robert A. III. Title. IV. Series.
QP321.S485  1994

612.7'4—dc20                                      94-21424
                                                  CIP
                                                  AC

ISBN 0-8050-2836-6
First Edition 1994

Printed in Mexico
All first editions are printed on acid-free paper ∞.
10 9 8 7 6 5 4 3 2 1

**Drawings by Lloyd Birmingham**

**Photo Credits**
Cover: Howard Sochurek/Woodfin Camp & Associates, Inc.
p. 10: M. I. Walker/Photo Researchers, Inc.; p. 11(t): Tom Branch/Photo Researchers, Inc.; p.
11(l): Art Directors/Phototake NYC; p. 11(r): Gérard Lacz/Animals Animals; p. 13: Jim
Carter/Photo Researchers, Inc.; p. 14: Francois Gohier/Photo Researchers, Inc.; p. 17(l): Bernard
Desestres/Agence Vandystadt/Photo Researchers, Inc.; p. 17(r): Tom and Pat Leeson/Photo
Researchers, Inc.; p. 19(tl)): A. Cosmos Blank/National Audubon Society/Photo Researchers, Inc.;
p. 19(br): NASA; p. 22: Jerome Wexler/Photo Researchers, Inc.; p. 23: Larry Simpson/Photo
Researchers, Inc.; p. 27: J. P. Ferrero/Jacana/Photo Researchers, Inc.; p. 36(tl) and 36(tr): Custom
Medical Stock Photo; p. 36(bl): M. Austerman/Animals Animals; p. 41: Jean-Marc
Giboux/Gamma-Liaison; p. 43(l): Lawrence Migdale/Photo Researchers, Inc.; p. 43(r): Andy
Levin/Photo Researchers, Inc.; p. 51: CNRI/Science Photo Library/Photo Researchers, Inc.; p. 53:
Richard Shock/Gamma Liaison; p. 54: K. R. Porter/Photo Researchers, Inc.; p. 55: Bard
Wrisley/Liaison International; p. 59: Science Photo Library/Photo Researchers, Inc.; p. 68: Edward
Drews/Photo Researchers, Inc.; p. 70: Joseph Nettis/Photo Researchers, Inc.; p. 71: Steve
Maslowski/Photo Researchers, Inc.; p. 73(bl): Art Stein/Photo Researchers, Inc.; p. 73(bc): Toni
Angermayer/Photo Researchers, Inc.; p. 73(br): Gamma Liaison; p. 77: Alan Levenson/Tony Stone
Worldwide; p. 79: Richard Hutchings/Photo Researchers, Inc.; p. 82: Tim Davis/Photo
Researchers, Inc.; p. 83: Jean-Marc Loubat/Agence Vandystadt/Photo Researchers, Inc.; p. 85:
Robert C. Burke/Liaison International; p. 87: Howard Sochurek/Woodfin Camp & Associates,
Inc.; p. 88: Fred McConnaughey/Photo Researchers, Inc.

# CONTENTS

# SECTION 1

# A WORLD OF MOTION

Fish swim through the water by swishing their tails. Snails creep along on a slimy trail that they make themselves. A horse gallops swiftly on four legs, while a duck waddles on two. An eagle soars through the air on powerful wings. All these animals have their own ways of moving. Special groups of cells called muscles help them all to move from place to place.

The muscles that we are most familiar with are called skeletal muscles. They work with the bones of the skeleton to help many animals, including humans, to move. It would be hard to think of anything we do that does not involve our muscles. We can walk, dance, play the piano, and throw a ball because our muscles can move our bones.

While you are sitting quietly reading this book, it may seem that you are moving only when you turn the page. But someone watching you would notice that your eyes darted back and forth as you focused on each line of print. Muscles make this possible. Meanwhile many muscles are making tiny adjustments to keep your body in a sitting position so that you do not fall over. You are barely aware of these muscle actions.

You are even less aware of other muscle activities that are going on constantly in your body. Can you feel your chest rising and falling as you breathe? If you place your hand in front of your mouth and nose, you will feel the puffs of air as you breathe out. Muscles help us to breathe.

Your heart is beating, pumping blood around your body. You can feel the blood pulsing along at your wrists and temples. The heart is a special muscle. There are also muscles in the blood vessels that carry the blood around the body.

Muscles help move food through your digestive system. Muscles in your mouth and throat help you to swallow. Muscles in your stomach churn up your food. Muscles squeeze food along through your intestines. Your tongue is mostly muscle, too, and it moves a lot when you talk and eat.

All of the muscles of the body make up the muscular system. It works closely with many other systems of the body. Your muscles are working when you are asleep and awake, helping to move parts of your body and to keep your internal organs doing the jobs they need to do to keep you alive and healthy.

# MUSCLES IN THE ANIMAL KINGDOM

The muscles that help animals to move their bodies are made up of thousands or even millions of cells that work together. These cells are special because they can contract, or shorten. All cells can contract, but muscle cells can do it better than most other cells. Muscle cells contain special proteins that help them to contract. Muscles allow animals to make many different movements. And yet each muscle cell itself can't do anything but contract. By contracting and relaxing, muscles are able to move the parts of an animal's body.

Single-celled animals can move, even though they don't have any muscles. The paramecium, a tiny single-celled pond creature, swims by waving tiny hairlike cilia back and forth like the oars of a rowboat. Another microscopic pond animal, the ameba, looks like a shapeless, colorless blob of jelly. But it can move, too, oozing after a swimming paramecium. Armlike bulges suddenly appear on the ameba's body and reach out toward the paramecium. When the ameba moves forward, its body actually flows into its new "arms." These bulges may close around the unlucky paramecium and capture it. Although these one-celled creatures do not have muscles, they contain the same kinds of proteins that help muscles to contract. These proteins help single-celled creatures to move.

In animals that are made up of many cells, different types of cells perform different functions. Some are best at carrying messages. Others are the experts in getting or digesting food for the body. Still others develop the ability to contract much better than the rest of the cells. It is these contracting specialists that form the muscles of animals.

Simple creatures may have simple kinds of muscles. In the sponge, for example, there are cells around the open-

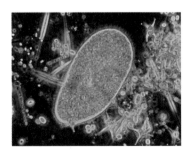

*This is a tiny paramecium living in plankton, which are even smaller water creatures.*

ing or "mouth" that work somewhat like a rubber band closing the top of a bag.

More complicated animals have a greater variety of muscles. The hydra, a pond animal that is hardly larger than a speck of dust, has a vase-shaped body, topped by a crown of waving tentacles with which it catches its prey. Rings of muscle allow it to close its mouth opening. Other muscles, which run along its body and tentacles, allow it to wave its tentacles, stuff prey into its mouth, and move about in the water.

*A pond hydra uses its tentacles to catch its food.*

A flatworm is made up of millions of cells, although it is barely the length of your thumbnail. It has the same types of muscles as the hydra, as well as muscles that help to change the shape of its body and to raise and turn its head. There are also muscles inside a flatworm's body that help it to breathe, digest its food, and bring sex cells together to start the lives of new flatworms.

A snail moves along on a rippling foot that is mainly muscle. Clams, too, move about on a muscular foot.

None of these creatures have skeletons. The muscles that help them to move are called **smooth muscles**. The muscles that help insects to move, on the other hand, are different. An insect's body is surrounded by a thick, armorlike skeleton. Its muscles are attached to parts of its skeleton to help it to move. These muscles are called **skeletal muscles**.

Animals with backbones, such as fish, amphibians, reptiles, birds, and mammals, have both smooth and skeletal muscles. They also have **cardiac muscle**, which makes up the walls of the heart. The muscular systems of these animals are surprisingly similar to ours. But each has adapted in its own special way, depending on how it moves about—its form of **locomotion**.

*Four-footed animals have muscular systems similar to ours, but each has developed its own way of moving about.*

# LOCOMOTION IN THE WATER

Scientists believe that the first animals that ever lived on our planet were water animals. Even today, all the major groups of animals have some members living in the oceans, lakes, ponds, or streams.

Some water dwellers, such as sponges and oysters, spend nearly all their lives anchored at the bottom, feeding on tiny bits of food that drift past them in the water. For these animals, life is often risky. An animal that can move about actively has great advantages. It does not have to wait for whatever dinner might happen to float by but can go out in search of its food. If danger threatens, it can move away and save itself.

Water is a denser substance than the air in which we live, and it helps to hold up things that are placed in it. This characteristic is called **buoyancy**. There is a limit, however, to the buoyant force of water. It can hold up light objects, like a cork, so that they bob and float at the surface. But denser objects, whose weight is greater than the buoyant force, sink through the water.

Many water dwellers use buoyancy to help them float at the surface of the water. Jellyfish drift along in the ocean currents, stinging and eating small swimming creatures that blunder by. Seals and whales also float while they nap at the surface of the water. A mother sea otter leaves her baby anchored to a floating cradle of seaweed while she hunts for food, and then she floats on her back, using her belly as a dinner plate. But seals, whales, and otters also have better ways of getting around in water than just floating. They can swim and dive, too.

If you know how to swim, very likely the first stroke you learned was the dog paddle. Floating on your stomach, you moved about by flapping your arms and legs back and forth. Some water animals also swim by pad-

*A sea otter is an expert swimmer and floats easily on its back as it enjoys a meal of crab.*

dling. The turtle is one of the champion paddlers of the animal kingdom. Its four legs are flattened like the paddles of a canoe, and it uses them in very much the same way.

The best swimmers, though, do not just paddle with their legs. They use their whole bodies to swim. Have you ever watched a goldfish swimming in a bowl? It does not paddle with its fins. Instead, it moves by smooth back-and-forth sweeps of its tail. The force of these sweeps runs all the way down the fish's body, and its backbone forms graceful S-shapes as it swims. The fish's fins are like the rudders of a boat—they help the fish to steer, and they also help to straighten it up if it starts to roll over. The sea mammals—whales, dolphins, and seals—swim in very much the same way as a fish, but the tail flukes of a whale or dolphin and the hind flippers of a seal move up and down instead of side to side.

Remember the tiny pond creature, the paramecium? It swims through the water by the action of thousands of tiny hairlike cilia, which wave back and forth in a perfectly coordinated rhythm. Another pond dweller, the euglena, is propelled by the lashing of a single long, whiplike flagellum. A frog pushes itself through the water by powerful kicks of its long hind legs. The squid uses a kind of jet propulsion. It squirts a jet of water out of one end of its body to move in the opposite direction.

The paramecium is a very fast swimmer for its size. But in actual speed,

*The tail flukes of the humpback whale move up and down to propel it through the water.*

larger animals can move much faster. This seems logical, for the larger the animal, the more muscles its body can hold, and the more powerful a force it can exert. A large fish can usually move faster than a smaller one. But this general rule holds only up to a certain limit. Some water animals are so large that the water itself resists their movement. This resistance rises faster than the "muscle power" as the size increases further. All the additional strength of the larger animal is used up just in fighting the increased resistance of the water. That is why the whale and the much smaller porpoise have the same swimming speed—about 20 to 25 miles (32 to 40 kilometers) an hour.

Not all water animals can swim. We have already mentioned some, such as the sponge and the oyster, that spend nearly all their lives in one place, attached to the bottom of the ocean. Others can move, but mainly along the solid surfaces of the bottom or the stalks and leaves of water plants. The clam, a close relative of the oyster, has a muscular foot, shaped like the blade of a hatchet. The clam sticks out its foot, and blood flows into it. The foot swells up, and the clam uses it as an anchor while it drags its heavy shell forward. Then it forces the blood back out of its foot to release the "anchor," and thrusts its foot forward again to inch along.

*A clam pulls itself slowly along by means of a muscular foot.*

foot of clam

# LOCOMOTION IN THE AIR

Have you ever wished you could fly like a bird? Although many people have tried to make wings that could help them to fly, a human being can never fly like a bird. Many different systems in a bird's body, including its muscular system, are specially adapted to its locomotion in the air. People are not built to fly through the air by flapping their arms, although we humans have been intelligent enough to build airplanes, helicopters, and rockets that can fly us about. Studies of how birds and other animals fly have helped and are still helping human engineers to build better airplanes.

In some ways, flying through the air is like swimming through water. Air has some buoyancy. It is not as great as the buoyancy of water, because air is not as dense. The buoyancy of air helps hold birds up when they are flying. Streams of air flowing past the birds' wings provide what scientists call lift. The bird flaps its feather-covered wings up and down to send it forward. The air presses against the wings on the downstroke, producing lift.

The bird needs powerful chest and wing muscles to keep its wings flapping. The enormous flight muscles in the breast of a bird may make up as much as a quarter of the weight of its body. The chest muscles of a man, in contrast, account for less than 1 percent of his weight.

Many systems of the bird's body are specially adapted for the needs of flight. The bones of birds are amazingly light because they are filled with many hollow spaces. The bird's efficient respiratory and circulatory systems help to keep the flight muscles supplied with food and oxygen.

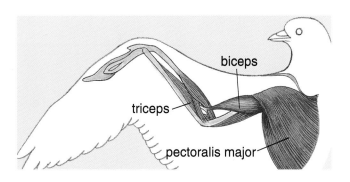

*A bird has powerful wing muscles attached to very lightweight bones.*

A number of different kinds of insects developed wings and the ability to fly long before there were birds. After birds appeared on the earth, a group of mammals, the bats, also developed a form of flight.

All three groups of flying animals have wings for flying. They all have well-developed muscular systems that provide for flapping these wings rapidly to produce thrust.

When you hear a bee or fly buzzing, this is the sound of its wings beating at astonishing speeds. A horsefly beats its wings 200 times a second, and a tiny midge can beat its wings more than 1,000 times a second. Usually the smaller an insect is, the faster it moves its wings. All this muscle activity uses up an enormous amount of energy, and many insects must spend much of their time eating to take in new fuel.

There is one type of flight that a human can master when fitted with the right pair of wings—gliding. This is a passive kind of flight in which the wings are held out stiff, and winds and air currents provide the lift and movement. The first airplanes were gliders.

The best gliders are birds. They may fly by flapping their wings a few times, then glide for a bit, using the gliding to save energy. Or they may soar through the air for hours, riding the winds and upward-rising columns of warm air.

Some land animals and even water animals have developed an ability to glide. The flying squirrel looks very much like a kite. Membranes connect its legs and body. When it stretches out these membranes, it can sail through the air from one tree branch to another. The flying fish also has a kind of "wings." It can leap out of the water and glide through the air for as much as 50 yards (46 meters).

*To build mechanical gliders, we have often followed the design of nature's best gliders, such as the bald eagle.*

# LOCOMOTION ON LAND

If life on our planet did begin in the water, the first animals that came out onto land had some very difficult adjustments to make. One of the most important of these involved the muscular system. Everything in our world is acted upon by the force of gravity. This force constantly pulls downward upon us, and we must work against it to hold ourselves upright.

An animal living on the land must use its muscles to hold up its full weight against the force of gravity. An animal in the water, on the other hand, has the water to help hold it up. As a result, a land animal must have stronger muscles than a water animal.

Scientists believe that one of the first animals to move onto land was a kind of fish that moved about by scraping along with its fins and tail and wiggling its body. The walking catfish is a living example of this kind of creature. It uses its fins as a crude sort of legs to move from one pond to another.

Most real land animals move about on two, four, six, eight, or even more legs. But there are a few land animals that seem to get along quite well without any legs at all. The earthworm and snake wiggle along by using their muscles to push against solid objects such as the ground. If you place a snake on a perfectly smooth pane of glass, it will not be able to move at all because it has nothing to brace itself against.

Most land animals have legs, and they move about by walking, running, or leaping. Support and balance are very important for these forms of locomotion. Four-legged animals have a much easier task than we humans, and six-legged insects are even better off.

When an insect is at rest, it rests on six legs, and its head and abdomen balance each end. When an insect walks, it lifts three legs at a time—the front and back leg on one side and the middle leg on the other. That leaves three legs still on the ground, as though the insect were sitting on a three-legged stool. As the insect moves, it picks up one triangle of legs and then the other in turn.

*The tiger beetle (above) with only six legs can travel much more easily than the robot explorer Dante 2 (right) can with eight legs. This spiderlike machine was developed to explore dangerous places, such as the inside of a volcano.*

A four-legged animal is also firmly supported and well balanced. When a dog walks, for example, it lifts only one foot at a time, leaving a triangle of three legs on the ground. It lifts each foot in turn, in a regular pattern. When the dog runs, it lifts its legs in the same order as when it walks, but it lifts the second leg before the first is back on the ground. Running requires much finer balance and coordination than walking. But it is much faster than walking. A cheetah, the fastest land animal, can run at a speed of 75 miles (120 kilometers) an hour!

Walking and running on two legs requires much better balance and coordination than moving about on four or six legs. When a two-legged animal walks, it lifts one foot at a time, and the weight of the whole body must be supported by the foot that remains on the ground. In running, part of the time both feet are off the ground at once!

Some pet dogs can be taught to walk on two legs, but they find it a difficult balancing act. Their bodies really aren't built for standing comfortably on two legs. Birds are well balanced for two-legged locomotion, with the head and tail at opposite ends helping to keep them stable. Bears can walk on their hind legs without much trouble because they carry most of their weight in the thick hind part of the body. Chimpanzees and gorillas, our closest animal relatives, can walk on two legs, but they often support part of their weight on their knuckles.

## CAN YOU JUMP AS WELL AS A FROG?

Some of the fastest animal runners actually use a combination of running and leaping to move so quickly. They push off from the ground with both hind legs to bound into the air, then come down on the two forelegs first, one after the other. The animals that are best at leaping, such as rabbits, frogs, and kangaroos, have hind legs that are much larger than their forelegs. Their hind legs have large, strong muscles, which can push off forcefully.

Which is the best leaper in the animal world? Well, a human broad jumper can leap about 11 feet (3.4 meters), and a kangaroo can jump 26 feet (8 meters). A tiny flea, the best jumper among the insects, can leap about 1 foot (30 centimeters). But let's compare those distances to the body size. A man can jump about twice his height. A kangaroo's jump covers about five times its height. But the tiny flea can leap *two hundred* times its body length!

Human beings are well equipped for two-legged locomotion. Our curved backbone and other parts of the skeleton support the body upright. Our muscles help to hold all the parts of the skeleton in place, and allow the legs and feet to hold up the weight of the whole body.

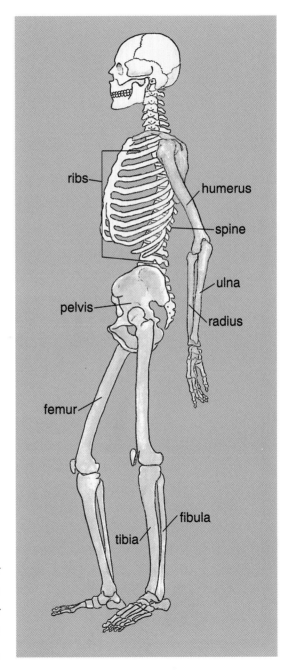

*The human skeleton is designed to work in cooperation with muscles to give us upright posture and motion.*

# MOVEMENT IN THE PLANT WORLD

Although plants cannot move their whole bodies, as animals do, they can and do move parts of their bodies—leaves, stems, flowers, or roots. We are not usually aware of these movements because they occur very slowly. But we can see their effects. Many plants open their leaves or flowers during the daytime and fold them up tight at night. If you turn a potted plant over on its side, it will soon bend so that its stem is again pointed upward and its root is pointed downward. If the tendrils of a pea plant touch the solid surface of a pole, they will curl around it.

Some plant movements are the result of growing. The stem of a plant turned on its side bends upward, for example, because its underside grows faster than its upper side. That happens because a plant hormone, a kind of chemical messenger called **auxin**, is pulled downward by gravity and accumulates on the underside of the plant. Auxin makes stems grow faster, so the stem soon turns upward. But the same hormone makes roots grow more slowly, and thus it causes the root to turn downward.

*A Venus flytrap*

Other plant movements are more similar to the ways animals move. The Venus flytrap has leaves that work like a spring trap. If an insect brushes against some bristly hairs on the leaf, it immediately snaps shut, trapping the insect so that it can be digested inside. The mimosa uses quick movements to avoid being eaten. If anything touches one of the tiny leaflets on a mimosa leaf, the whole leaf rapidly folds up tight. If the touch is strong enough, the leaf goes limp. An animal, seeing the drooping leaves, may be fooled into thinking the plant is sick and would not be good to eat.

Plants do not have an organized system of muscles as animals do. But special proteins like those that allow animal muscles to contract can help plants to move. They work by changing the **turgor**, or firmness, of the plant cells. Normally, plant cells are filled with water, which keeps them plump and firm. Plants draw water up through their roots and lose water through tiny openings in their leaves. If too much water is lost, the plant cells go limp. That is why houseplants wilt if you forget to water them.

At the base of each leaflet of the mimosa there is a little swelling, filled with water. There is a larger swelling at the base of each leaf, where it is attached to the stem. The water inside these swellings is held by proteins similar to the contracting chemicals in muscle cells, in the form of a jellylike compound. When something touches a mimosa leaflet, the proteins react and let go of their water, which drains out of the joint, making the leaf droop. The Venus flytrap works in a similar way. Muscle proteins are also involved when plants raise or lower their flowers and leaves or turn them toward the sun.

*Flowers cannot move from place to place, but with the help of muscle proteins they can turn toward the sun.*

## WATCHING PLANTS MOVE

Set up a pot with a bean plant in front of a white posterboard, ruled off in one-inch squares. Carefully note the positions of the leaves several times each day. The bean plant raises its leaves during the day and lowers them at night. You can make a "movie" by taking a photograph of the plant every 20 minutes. Be sure to have the camera in exactly the same place each time. Put the photos in a stack (in order), hold one side firmly, and run your thumb along the edges of the other side to show each photo in quick succession.

thumb flips photos

# SECTION 2

# DISCOVERING OUR MUSCULAR SYSTEM

Human beings have always been fascinated with motion. In ancient times, people believed that things such as the stars and the seas and the wind were alive, partly because they could move. Early people may not have understood that muscles are responsible for movement of living animals, but they made good use of their muscles.

Muscles are the body's machines for working. Long ago, people used their muscles to handle tools and to push or pull machines such as plows and sleds. About 6,000 years ago, oxen and other animals were probably used for the first time to pull plows.

About 2,400 years ago, Aristotle, the great Greek philosopher, wrote about how animals move. He described the way the limbs moved, and then explained it in mathematical terms. He pointed out that in order for an animal to walk erect, it must shift its weight around its center of gravity—an imaginary point around which the animal's weight is equally distributed. People's legs are so much stronger than their arms because the legs have to bear the weight of the body.

Five hundred years later, a Greek physician named Galen made many observations about the way muscles worked. He was the first to show that muscles contracted to pull on bones. He pointed out that muscles worked in pairs. When one muscle contracted, another muscle relaxed and became longer, so that the bone would be allowed to move. Galen also tried to describe what made muscles move. He pointed out that there were two different kinds of nerves. Some nerves carried messages from the brain or spinal cord to make muscles move. Other nerves carried messages from the body's sensory organs to the brain. But Galen believed that the messages that caused muscles to become shorter were "animal spirits."

Leonardo da Vinci was a famous fifteenth-century Italian artist and scientist. To study how muscles worked, he constructed models. He attached wires to a skeleton in places where muscles are attached in the body. Then he drew in great detail how the shape of the muscles changed to make different movements.

The seventeenth-century Dutch naturalist Antonie van Leeuwenhoek was the first to observe many things under the microscope. He looked at skeletal muscles under his microscopes and saw stripes in the tiny muscle fibers. He guessed correctly that these stripes had something to do with the way muscles contract.

In 1700 an Italian physician named Giorgio Baglivi pointed out that there were two kinds of muscles. Skeletal muscles were designed for sudden actions. But smooth muscles worked more slowly and for much longer.

During the late 1700s the Italian scientist Luigi Galvani discovered that electricity, traveling from nerves to muscles, caused the muscles of a frog's leg to contract.

In the late 1800s scientists learned more about the individual cells that make up muscles. Around the same time, more understanding was gained about motion. Using photography, scientists were able to see clearly for the first time how animals really moved. In 1878, for example, it was proven that when a horse gallops, its legs move so quickly that all four hooves are sometimes in the air at once!

*A horse has powerful muscles to help it move quickly.*

During the middle and later twentieth century, scientists learned much more about the chemical and electrical reactions that go on inside muscle cells to make them contract.

# OUR MUSCULAR SYSTEM

There are more than 650 muscles in your body. If you weigh about 80 pounds (36 kilograms), your body probably contains close to 40 pounds (18 kilograms) of muscle. It is a good thing that your body is nearly half muscle, because almost everything you do requires the use of muscles.

Muscles are the engines or machines that make your body go. They turn energy into a force, which produces movement. When the force of muscles moves the whole body, it is called locomotion. Often muscles move only parts of the body, as in winking your eye, kicking your leg, or the rising and falling of your chest when you breathe. Muscles also move various fluids and other materials through channels of the body—blood through the circulatory system, food through the digestive tract, and urine through the urinary tract.

Humans, like other animals, have three different kinds of muscles in their bodies. Skeletal muscles are often attached to bones and help to move parts of the body. They also give the body shape and hold our skeletons together.

Cardiac muscle makes up most of the heart. *Cardiac* comes from a word meaning "heart." The strong contractions of this muscle keep the heart beating on and on, from long before we are born until the moment we die.

The third type of muscle is called smooth muscle because the tiny muscle cells that compose it look very smooth under a microscope. Smooth muscles are found in many parts of the body: in the walls of blood vessels; in most of the organs in the body, including the kidneys, liver, and spleen; and in the digestive tract.

All three types of muscles have a special ability in common—they can all contract far more effectively than any other kinds of cells. But there are important differences in the way they act. Skeletal muscles get tired after only a few minutes. The smooth muscles of your blood vessels or intestines, however, can remain contracted for several hours. And your heart muscle goes on working steadily day after day for your entire life.

A large part of your face, legs, arms, neck, chest, and abdomen is made of muscles. The muscles of the body are many different sizes and shapes, depending on the job they need to do. The muscles of the eyes, for example, are small and not very strong. But the muscles in the thighs need to support the weight of the body, and so they are big and strong.

A typical muscle is wider in the middle and tapers at the ends. But there are many other muscle shapes. The muscles that run around the front of the abdomen to protect our internal organs are flat, like sheets. Some muscles are very thin and long. Others are shaped like feathers or rings, or look like thick blocks or thin triangles.

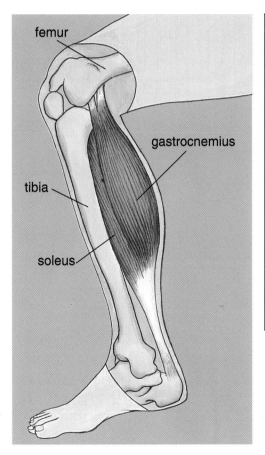

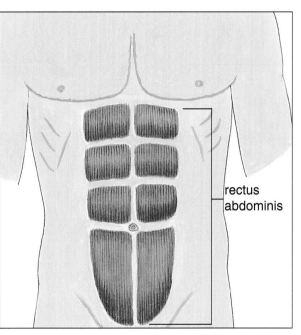

*The gastrocnemius muscle (left) and the rectus abdominis muscle (above) are two examples of skeletal muscle.*

# SKELETAL MUSCLES

Your entire skeleton is covered with muscles. The combined weight of your muscles is about three times as much as that of your bones. In fact, muscles weigh more than any other type of tissue in the body. Skeletal muscles allow you to move your arms, legs, hands, and other body parts. Skeletal muscles surround the mouth cavity and form most of the tongue. They surround the body cavities and separate the chest and abdomen. Skeletal muscles attached to the outer layer of the eyeball move the eyes.

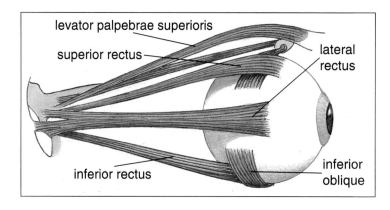

levator palpebrae superioris

superior rectus

lateral rectus

inferior rectus

inferior oblique

*The muscles that move the eye do not have to be nearly as strong as the muscles that move our large bones.*

Although many skeletal muscles pull on bones, they are not attached to them directly. Muscles are connected to bones by tough, whitish, cordlike tissues called **tendons**. The muscle pulls on the tendon, and the tendon in turn pulls on the bone. Tendons are very strong tissues, and they can stand up to the daily pulling and tugging as we use our muscles. You can feel one important tendon in the back of your ankle, right above the heel. This is the **Achilles tendon**. If you point your toe and then bend your foot up, you can feel your Achilles tendon tightening and relaxing.

Not all skeletal muscles link up with bones. Some skeletal muscles are attached to other muscles. Some are attached to the skin. But each skeletal muscle is attached in at least two places. When it contracts, the body parts to which it is attached are usually brought closer together.

Since skeletal muscles work closely with the bones, it is not surprising that they are divided into two groups, just as bones are. **Axial muscles** include those of the head, neck, and trunk. The muscles of the arms and legs are **appendicular muscles**.

There are 656 skeletal muscles in the human body, and each of them has a name. Some are named for the place in the body where they are found. *Brachii* indicates that a muscle is in the arm—for example, the biceps brachii and triceps brachii. The biceps brachii is the skeletal muscle that most people think of first when the word *muscle* is mentioned. It is the bulge of the upper arm that people show off when "making a muscle." *Pectoralis* means "of the chest," and *intercostal* means "between the ribs."

Muscles may also be named for their size, shape, or structure. The deltoid muscle in your shoulder is triangle-shaped, and it is named for the Greek letter *delta*, which is also shaped like a triangle. The trapezius muscle in your back has a four-sided trapezoid shape. Many muscles have names that include the words *maximus* ("largest"), *minimus* ("smallest"), *longus* ("long"), or *brevis* ("short").

Muscle names may also show their action. A **flexor** is a muscle that flexes (bends) a limb at a joint. The corresponding **extensor** muscle extends or straightens the limb at the same joint. A **sphincter** is a ring-shaped muscle whose contractions narrow the opening of the ring.

Skeletal muscles can exert tremendous power, but like a high-speed engine, a skeletal muscle cannot work for too long at a time. After a short time it must rest.

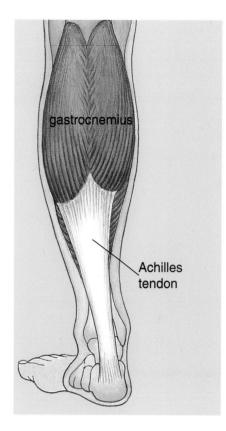

*The Achilles tendon is the strongest tendon in the body. It attaches the calf muscle to the heel bone. If the tendon is torn, you can barely walk and you cannot run.*

# SKELETAL MUSCLES WORK IN PAIRS

Bend your arm up. The **biceps muscle** in your upper arm contracts to pull up your arm. When you want to stretch your arm out straight, though, the biceps cannot work to straighten it out. Muscles can only pull, they cannot push. That's why many skeletal muscles work in pairs. The triceps muscle on the underside of the forearm helps to straighten the arm. When one muscle contracts, the other muscle relaxes. Muscle pairs are called **antagonists** because they work against each other. If your biceps muscle did not have an antagonist, you would have to lean over and let gravity slowly pull your forearm down in order to straighten it out.

We can make many different types of movements because in addition to working in pairs, a muscle's work is coordinated with a whole group of muscles. Certain muscles in a group contract to various degrees, while others relax. A particular muscle's role may vary, depending on the movement. Most movements involve more than one set of muscles. However, even when only a single part of the body is moved, other muscles have to contract to keep other body parts in place.

The biceps is a typical-looking skeletal muscle. It is thin at the ends and round in the middle. The rounded part is called the **belly**. One end is attached to a bone that moves. This end is called the **insertion**. The other end, called the **origin**, is attached to a bone that does not move.

The biceps and triceps both have their origin at the shoulder, but they have opposite effects because they are inserted in different places. When the biceps (a flexor muscle) contracts, it pulls on a bone in the inner part of the forearm, and the arm bends. When the triceps (an extensor muscle) contracts, it pulls on a bone in the outer part of the forearm, and the arm straightens.

The way a muscle works can be compared to a mechanical **lever**. A lever is a simple machine that makes tasks easier. A rigid rod rests on a pivot called a **fulcrum**. When force is applied to one part of the rod, a weight placed on another part of the rod is lifted. In our bodies, muscles supply the force to move bones, which correspond to the rod in a lever. The weight placed on the rod may be a part of the body to be moved, an object to be lifted, or both.

You can see for yourself how a lever works. Tie one end of a cord around the top of a 10-pound (4.5-kilogram) bag of potatoes, and make a loop in the other end of the cord. Holding the loop, try to lift the bag of potatoes. Now place the bag on a chair and tighten the loop around one end of a mop handle. Rest the mop handle on the back of the chair, parallel to the floor, and press down on the other end. Notice how much easier it is to lift the bag.

There are three different kinds of levers. A first-class lever is a typical "see-saw." Force is applied at one end, and the weight is at the other. The fulcrum is between them. Nodding your head uses a first-class lever. In a second-class lever, the fulcrum is at one end, the force is exerted at the other end, and the object to be lifted is in between. When you stand on your toes, the calf muscle at the back of your lower leg lifts your heel. This is a second-class lever. A third-class lever has its fulcrum at one end and the weight to be lifted at the other end; the force is exerted between them. The biceps pulls on the bones of the forearm in this way.

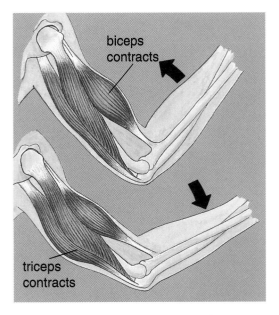

*Since muscles can only pull, they must work in pairs to give the body movement.*

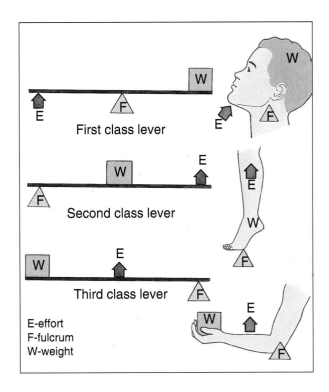

# BODY MOVEMENTS
# AND POSTURE

All animals that hold themselves up on legs and move about are constantly struggling against gravity. The skeleton is firm and rigid and provides some support. But if the body and limbs were completely firm and rigid, we wouldn't be able to move. That's why animal bodies are designed with movable joints between bones. But each joint is a weak spot, and it must be held together and supported by muscles. Muscles and bones work together to provide for support and movement of the body and its parts.

Have your parents ever reminded you to "stand up straight" or not to slump over in your chair? Good posture is an important key to feeling well and keeping your body ready for all of the activities in your daily life.

In order for you to maintain an upright posture, your muscles are constantly making adjustments. You might think that no muscles need to work when you are just standing still. Yet if you try to stand for a while, you will find yourself growing tired. Muscles are contracting, pulling on your bones and other muscles to keep you balanced.

You can test for yourself how one set of muscles helps you to stand. Sit on a chair with your feet resting lightly on the floor. Feel the back of your calf. The muscle there is called the **gastrocnemius muscle**. While you are sitting, and your legs are not supporting you, the gastrocnemius muscle is soft and relaxed. Now stand up, and reach down to feel the back of your calf again. It is hard and firm. The gastrocnemius muscle is contracting, helping to support the weight of your whole body. You can feel it contract even more if you rise up on your toes.

An important key to understanding both posture and locomotion is the center of gravity. Gravity is constantly pulling down on objects—this is what makes things have weight. For a sphere, the center of gravity would be exactly in the center of the object. But for objects of other shapes, this is not necessarily so. When the center of gravity is well supported, the forces acting upward counteract the downward pull of gravity. In our bodies these upward forces are exerted by contracting muscles. If the center of gravity is shifted, muscles must compensate for the changes to keep the body from toppling over. For example, wearing high heels shifts a person's center of gravity forward. That's why women who wear high heels tend to lean backward with the upper part of their bodies. Walking or running constantly changes a person's center of gravity, so muscles in the legs, back, and neck must constantly make adjustments.

## WHY DO PEOPLE SLEEP LYING DOWN?

When you lie down, your body is supported in many places, so it is the easiest posture to maintain. If you've ever fallen asleep sitting in a chair, you may have noticed you woke up with a stiff neck or some other sign that your muscles were straining to maintain your posture while you slept.

Too much bed rest is not good, though. When muscles and bones are not used regularly, they get weaker. After a few weeks in bed, you would not even be able to stand up without holding on to something!

Good posture is not a stiff military "standing at attention" position. It is a relaxed position that will allow you to change quickly into any desired movement. The best posture for each person is one in which the parts of the body are balanced with the most support and the least amount of strain. In a correct standing posture the head is held high and balanced easily on the neck, the abdomen is held in, and the chest is allowed to expand freely. The shoulders are not allowed to sag forward, and the arms hang freely. Good posture is developed gradually—a small child tends to stand with abdomen forward, while the upper body leans backward to compensate.

Our upright posture has brought many benefits for humans. The main one is that the hands are free to carry and manipulate things. But many

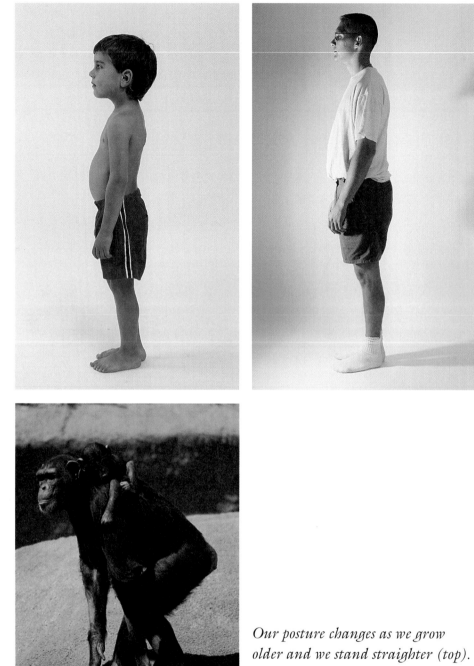

*Our posture changes as we grow older and we stand straighter (top). A chimpanzee's normal posture (left) has a forward thrust.*

people do not have good posture. Minor differences are not usually a problem. In fact, you can often recognize someone from the way he or she stands or walks. But if the posture is too far from the "correct" position, the body is not able to move efficiently. This can cause backaches and even deformities.

Support and balance are the main factors in locomotion, just as they are in maintaining good posture. The complicated sequence of movements involved in walking or running becomes so automatic that you hardly ever have to think about them. Yet it took a lot of practice when you were a baby. First you crept on your belly like a reptile. Then you crawled on your hands and knees. Finally, you pulled yourself up to an upright position and tottered and tumbled many times before you were able to walk.

# MUSCLE CELLS

Pick up a pencil. In this simple action, muscles of your hand and arm are working. Although you may see some of these muscles bulging as they contract, the actual work of a muscle is done by millions of individual muscle cells, each too small to be seen, which work together as a team.

Just as there are three types of muscles, there are three basic kinds of muscle cells in the body: smooth, skeletal, and cardiac muscle cells. All muscle cells are more or less elongated, or stretched out, which is why they are usually referred to as **muscle fibers**. But there are many differences among the three types of muscle fibers, in the size and shape of the cells, and in the way they are arranged in the muscle tissue.

Skeletal muscle fibers are shaped like a cylinder or a long rod. They are rather unusual cells. Most cells have a single nucleus (the cell's "control center"). But skeletal muscle cells have as many as 100 or more nuclei. These nuclei are not buried deep inside the cell as in other body cells. Instead, they are found on the outside of the fiber, just under the thin membrane that covers the cell. Under a microscope, skeletal muscle cells seem to be striped, marked by a series of dark and light bands that repeat in a regular pattern. That is why skeletal muscle is also called **striated muscle** (*striated* means "striped").

Individual skeletal muscle fibers are wrapped in a connective tissue covering. Groups of skeletal muscles are gathered into bundles, which are wrapped in another sheet of connective tissue. The muscle itself is a bundle of bundles, wrapped in yet another layer of thick connective tissue.

Each skeletal muscle fiber runs the entire length of the muscle. In some muscles, the fibers are more than a foot (30 centimeters) long! And unlike other body cells, skeletal muscle fibers may be visible without a micro-

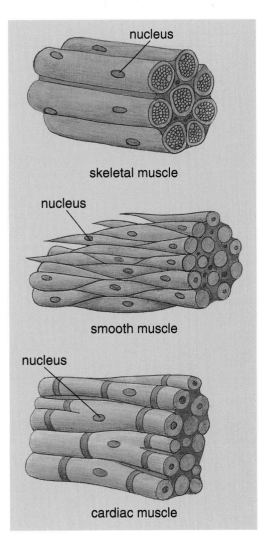

nucleus

skeletal muscle

nucleus

smooth muscle

nucleus

cardiac muscle

*This drawing shows the basic structure of the three different muscle-fiber bundles.*

scope. Each muscle fiber in a bundle is made up of a bundle of thinner threads called **myofibrils**. And every myofibril contains thousands of even thinner **myofilaments**. Skeletal muscle cells appear striped because some of the myofilaments are thick and some are thin, and they overlap each other. The thick filaments contain a protein called **myosin**. The thin filaments contain another protein, **actin**. These special "contractile" proteins help the muscle cell contract.

A smooth muscle cell is smaller. It is narrow at the ends and bulging in the middle. It has a single nucleus, buried deep inside. Each muscle fiber is wrapped in connective tissue. Smooth muscle cells are arranged parallel to each other, in cords, bundles, tubes, sheets, or pouches, with their narrow ends overlapping other muscle fibers. In the stomach, bladder, and other hollow organs, there are two layers of smooth muscle sheets. One makes up the outside wall of the organ and the other the inside. In blood vessels, smooth muscle fibers wrap around the walls like threads on a spool. Each cell membrane is joined with the fibers around it.

Smooth muscle fibers contain the special contractile proteins, actin and myosin. But the filaments do not overlap each other in the same way as in skeletal muscle cells, so the cells do not appear striped.

Cardiac muscle cells are striped like skeletal muscle fibers. But unlike skeletal muscle cells, they usually have a single nucleus buried inside each fiber. Cardiac muscle fibers branch and merge into surrounding fibers to form an interconnected network.

Skeletal muscles contain two types of fibers: **fast-twitch** and **slow-twitch fibers**. Fast-twitch fibers are large cells, each made up of many myofibrils. They contract quickly, providing short bursts of energy. This makes them important for strength and power.

In some animals, such as chickens, fast-twitch and slow-twitch fibers are separated. Fast-twitch fibers make up the white meat of a chicken. Slow-twitch fibers make up the dark meat of a chicken. Slow-twitch fibers are smaller cells with fewer myofibrils. They contract slowly and steadily and are important for activities that require endurance. Slow-twitch fibers give the muscles that contain them a rich red color because they contain a rich supply of **myoglobin**, a pigment similar to the hemoglobin that makes red blood cells red.

## ARE GREAT ATHLETES BORN WITH THE RIGHT MUSCLES?

Muscle fibers cannot be converted from one type to another. Researchers have found that in general, those who excel in long-distance races have many more slow-twitch muscle fibers than fast-twitch fibers. Sprinters have much higher levels of fast-twitch fibers.

In humans, all skeletal muscles contain both types of fibers, but in different amounts. White fibers are involved in delicate and skilled movements. In our bodies these fibers are concentrated in such muscles as the biceps and the muscles that move the eyeball. Red fibers are found mostly in muscles involved with breathing and eating. Red fibers are also important in maintaining posture, which requires long, slow contractions.

*The many slow-twitch muscle fibers of a long-distance runner contract slowly and steadily to give the runner endurance.*

# VOLUNTARY AND INVOLUNTARY MUSCLES

Skeletal muscles are often called **voluntary muscles**, because you can control their actions voluntarily, by your own will. Using skeletal muscles, you can raise your hand, open it, close it, nod your head, kick your foot, and turn around in a circle. The muscles that move all these body parts do what you want them to, when you want them to.

But you cannot control the action of smooth muscles, no matter how hard you try. You cannot tell your stomach to churn harder or open the blood vessels in your legs wider or squeeze your spleen into a tight ball, just by wanting to. Because the smooth muscles cannot be controlled by the will, they are called **involuntary muscles**.

Some actions can be controlled by either voluntary or involuntary muscles. Blink your eyes. That was a controlled action; you blinked because you wanted to. Now ask a friend to wave his or her hand in front of your eyes when you are not expecting it. (Be careful!) When your friend's hand waves, you will probably blink, even though you may not have wanted to. Blinking can be an automatic, involuntary action that helps to protect the eyes from damage. It is fortunate that the eyelids are supported by smooth muscles, for if you had to think each time before blinking, you might be blinded by some flying object before you had time to react. People also blink automatically a number of times each minute, even when nothing is threatening their eyes. This action helps to keep the eyeballs moist.

Cardiac muscle is another type of involuntary muscle. You cannot make your heart beat faster just by telling it to. But there are some ways to control your heart muscle indirectly. Running up a flight of stairs will make your heart beat faster. In fact, just standing up will speed up your heartbeat. You can even make your heartbeat speed up by thinking about something very exciting or frightening. Some people have trained themselves to control involuntary actions like heartbeat and breathing by indirect methods.

After we are born, we slowly learn to use our skeletal muscles to move. A baby learns to lift its head and eventually how to hold a cup, crawl, and walk. As we grow we learn how to tie our shoes and to do complicated things like paint a portrait, play the piano, or perform a dance routine.

*Learning to crawl (above) is a gradual process of learning to control muscles. Practice will add to muscle control and will make dance movements (right) become more routine.*

Learning to do new things such as riding a bike or playing the piano takes a lot of practice. You have to learn how to control your muscles to make the right movements. At first you may be very slow because you have to think about each movement. Your brain has to organize which bones and muscles to use, and in what order. But if you keep practicing, you get much quicker, and you don't have to think as much about what you are doing.

# CONTROLLING MOVEMENT

How does your brain tell your muscles what to do? It sends messages to the body through **motor nerves**. These thin nerve fibers, like tiny threads, begin in the brain and run down the spine. From there they branch out to every part of the body. The branching nerves end in tiny buttonlike nerve endings called **motor end plates**. Each of these fits into a hollow on the surface of a muscle fiber. The connection between the nerve ending and the muscular fiber is called a **neuromuscular junction**. Each neuron (nerve cell) with the muscle fibers it controls is referred to as a **motor unit**.

When the brain sends electrical signals along the nerve fibers to the muscles, the chemical balance inside the muscle cells is changed, causing the muscle fiber to tighten, or contract. The messages tell the muscles when, how much, and how long to contract.

For every movement that we make, the brain must arrange for the proper muscles to contract in the correct timing sequence with the action

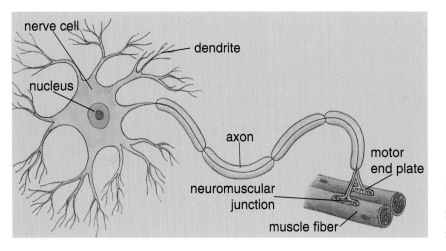

*The brain sends messages to muscles by means of motor nerves.*

of other muscles. Even simple tasks require a lot of coordinating. Walking uses more than 100 muscles!

Our senses of sight, hearing, smell, touch, and taste provide the brain with information to guide our movements. But information is also sent by the muscles themselves. Sensory organs called **proprioceptors** are spread throughout skeletal muscles, tendons, joints, and in the inner ear to keep the brain aware of body movements and the positions of the limbs. In the muscles, proprioceptors called **muscle spindles** send messages to the brain when the muscle fibers stretch. This lets the brain know how contracted a muscle is. Muscles that perform very fine movements contain more muscle spindles.

Proprioceptors play an important role in **reflex actions**. A reflex is any quick automatic response that the body makes every time a certain thing occurs. The thing that provokes the reflex reaction is called a **stimulus**. Your pupils, for example, automatically get smaller when a bright light shines on them. You pull your hands away from a hot surface without having to think about it. While you are sitting, groups of muscles are reflexively contracting and relaxing to maintain your posture.

When a child is first born, there are several motor neurons joining with each muscle fiber. As we grow and become better able to control our muscles, fewer connections are needed. Eventually there is only one motor neuron for a whole group of muscle fibers. A single message causes all the fibers in the group to contract.

There are an average of 150 muscle fibers in each motor unit in our bodies. The motor neurons that bring messages to muscles in the hand control much smaller groups of muscle fibers. That way the muscles are able to perform delicate and coordinated activities, such as threading a needle. There are as few as three muscle fibers in a motor unit in the tiny muscles of the eye. The muscles in the legs are large and strong. The motor neurons there control larger groups of muscle fibers, because delicate movements are not required. There may be 1,000 or more muscle fibers in each motor unit in the slow-moving calf muscle.

The brain cells that control body movements are found in the **motor strips**, two bands of cells running down the sides of the brain. Two-thirds of each motor strip are involved in moving just the hands and the mouth. That is not too surprising—the movements involved in speaking and using our hands are two of the most important tasks for the human muscular system.

# MUSCLE CELL CONTRACTIONS

When a muscle cell **contracts**, it does not contract only partway. As soon as a strong enough signal reaches it, the muscle cell contracts as much as it can. Scientists call this kind of action the "all or none law." A muscle cell contracts either completely or not at all.

How, then, can you hold an ice-cream cone without crushing it? The answer is that the "all or none law" describes the action of single skeletal muscle *cells* but not of whole skeletal *muscles*. A muscle is made up of millions of muscle cells. The amount a whole muscle contracts depends on how many of its cells are contracting. More muscle cells must contract to lift a 5-pound (2.2-kilogram) weight than to lift a 1-pound (0.45-kilogram) weight. And even more muscle cells must contract to lift a 10-pound (4.5-kilogram) weight. When you walk slowly, only some of the muscle fibers in your leg muscles contract. But when you run, many more muscle fibers are stimulated. Muscles contract smoothly because the muscle fibers in a single motor unit are not all clumped together but are scattered over a large area of the muscle.

An individual muscle cell cannot stay contracted for very long—only a fraction of a second. Its action is therefore a tiny twitch. But you can keep your muscles contracted for long periods, for example, when you are holding up a heavy weight. You can do this because different groups of muscle cells are stimulated in turn. The action of a muscle is something like a relay race, in which the contractions of one group of cells take over when the contractions of another group stop, to keep the contraction of the whole muscle going.

After a muscle cell contracts, it must have a little time to recover before it is able to contract again. During this period it seems to "breathe"—it takes in oxygen carried to it by blood cells in the nearby capillaries, and it gives off carbon dioxide and heat. If the signals coming to a muscle call for a very strong contraction, or a very long one, each muscle cell will be stimulated again and again. It may need to contract again before it has had time to recover completely from its last contraction. If this occurs, the muscle gradually grows tired, and the twitches of its individual cells grow weaker and finally stop. Have you ever tried to hold something that was so heavy that you finally dropped it? Your muscles grew tired, or **fatigued**. If a fatigued muscle is allowed to rest for a while, it will soon be able to contract again.

Normally, the muscles of the body are not completely relaxed. At any particular time, some of the cells in each muscle are contracted. The slight contraction of the whole muscle that results is called **muscle tone**. Muscle tone is important to maintain posture and hold up the head. It also helps

*It takes a number of strong muscles to hold up the head, which is actually quite heavy. The average adult brain alone weighs about 3 pounds (1.3 kilograms).*

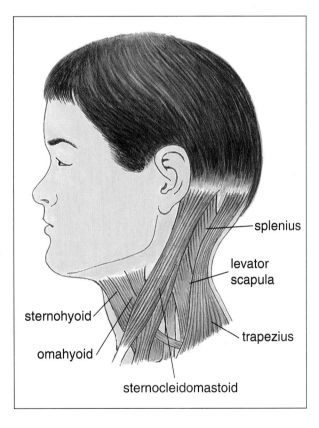

splenius

levator scapula

sternohyoid

omahyoid

trapezius

sternocleidomastoid

## SMOOTH MUSCLE CONTRACTIONS

Smooth muscles have been harder to study because not all smooth muscles respond to stimuli in the same way. But in general, smooth muscles contract more slowly and with less force than skeletal muscles. Smooth muscles can remain contracted for long periods of time without fatigue. We are usually completely unaware of smooth muscle contractions. But sometimes they make themselves felt painfully as in hunger pangs (stomach contractions), the intestinal cramps that may accompany diarrhea, and the powerful contractions of the uterus during childbirth.

In skeletal muscles, each individual motor unit must be stimulated before it will contract. But when one smooth muscle fiber is stimulated, the surrounding fibers also contract, so that the entire muscle contracts together. Smooth muscle can also contract effectively even when it is stretched out. Thus, the stomach can still contract when it is filled with food and the bladder when filled with urine, for example. Skeletal muscle cannot contract properly when it is stretched out.

to keep the muscle cells "in practice" so that they will be able to work effectively when the muscle is called upon to work. Our muscles have the least amount of muscle tone when we are sleeping. Only a small number of fibers are contracting then. Muscle tone increases when we are nervous or anxious.

Our muscles do not always shorten when they contract. Have you ever tried to lift a box that was too heavy to budge? Your arm muscles tensed, but they could not shorten. This kind of contraction is called an **isometric contraction**. (*Isometric* comes from the Greek for "constant length.") Perhaps you have heard of isometric exercises. These are exercises that tense muscles without actually moving parts of the body, such as standing in a doorway and pushing against the sides of the door frame. **Isotonic contractions** occur when muscles shorten as they contract.

## CARDIAC MUSCLE CONTRACTIONS

Cardiac muscle is similar to smooth muscle because of its rhythmic contractions, but the internal structure of cardiac muscle fibers is similar to a skeletal muscle fiber. Like smooth muscle fibers, cardiac muscle fibers do not contract alone. Stimulation of one cell quickly spreads to the surrounding cells. In skeletal muscle an individual muscle fiber is either contracted or not, but the whole muscle can be contracted a little or a lot. In cardiac muscle the entire muscle has an all-or-nothing response. Normally the heart contractions follow one another in a regular rhythm of about 72 per minute.

# HOW A MUSCLE CELL CONTRACTS

If the proteins actin and myosin are removed from muscle cells and placed in a drop of salt solution on a microscope slide, and a bit of a chemical called adenosine triphosphate (ATP) is added, a fascinating thing will happen—the protein fibers will contract. This can be seen under a microscope. In experiments such as these, as well as observations of living muscle cells, scientists have learned a great deal about how muscles work. But some mysteries still remain.

Biologists today believe that the **sliding filament theory**, first proposed in 1950, is a good description of what happens to make muscles contract. In very highly magnified pictures taken in an electron microscope, it can be seen that the myosin filaments look rather like two-headed snakes, with a long body (or tail) and two thickened heads attached to branches (arms) at one end. The arms that hold the heads are hinged, so that the heads can be drawn in close or stick out to the sides.

In a muscle cell, the thicker myosin filaments are surrounded by thinner actin filaments. Both types lie lengthwise along the muscle fiber, arranged so that only the ends of the two types of filaments overlap when the muscle cell is relaxed. This is the reason for the striped appearance of the muscle cell under the microscope: the places where the two kinds of filaments overlap look very dark, those that contain only myosin filaments look a little lighter, and the places where there are only thin actin filaments are very light. There are also some narrow dark bands where the actin filaments are linked together.

Along each actin filament there is a series of "active sites"—spots that are capable of reacting chemically. In a relaxed muscle cell these active sites have a protective covering that prevents them from reacting. But when the muscle fiber is stimulated, the active sites are uncovered. At the end of the filament, which overlaps with myosin, some active sites attract myosin heads, which spring out to form **cross-bridges**, attached to actin. But then further changes occur, and the heads bend inward, pulling the actin along the myosin filament. The heads then break away and snap out to a perpendicular position again. That brings them close to other active sites, farther along on the actin filament.

The sliding process repeats: the cross-bridges attach, the heads tilt inward, pulling the actin filament farther in along the myosin, and then the heads break away and snap out again, ready to attach farther along. The process continues until the actin filaments have been pulled in as far as they can go, and the ends of successive myosin filaments are touching. Some scientists call this sliding process the "walk-along" theory because the myosin heads seem to walk along the actin filaments. Others describe it as a "ratchet" mechanism, similar to the working of a ratchet wrench.

*In this section of striated cardiac muscle, the myofilaments appear as fine, pink vertical stripes.*

When the brain stops sending messages for the muscle to contract, the actin and myosin filaments pull away from each other. As each muscle fiber relaxes, the entire muscle becomes longer, until it is relaxed.

How long does all this take? A muscle contraction usually lasts for 0.01 to 0.04 second. Then the muscle cell relaxes for a somewhat longer time—up to 0.5 second.

## BELIEVE IT OR NOT . . .

The "sliding filament theory," which explained how the special chemicals in muscle cells worked together to make the cells contract, was announced in 1950. Two teams of scientists, working independently, had come up with the same theory at the same time. One team, at M.I.T. in Cambridge, Massachusetts, was headed by the American researcher Hugh Huxley. The other team, at Cambridge University in England, was headed by an English researcher named Andrew Huxley.

# FUEL FOR MUSCLES

Cars need gasoline to run their engines. The "fuel" that runs your television set is electricity. Our bodies need fuel to operate, too. We get it from the foods that we eat. The main fuel the body uses is a type of simple sugar called **glucose**. There is a steady supply of glucose in our blood and in the tissues of the body.

**Glycogen** is an energy source that is stored in the muscles and liver. Glycogen is made up of thousands of glucose molecules joined together. When extra glucose is needed, glycogen is broken down into glucose molecules and delivered to the body cells in the bloodstream.

Fat is also a fuel for the body. It is stored in special fat cells. When other body fuels are running low, fat molecules are broken down into simpler parts, which are delivered by the bloodstream to the muscles to be used for energy.

The body stores much of the chemical energy from glucose and the other body fuels in a more readily usable form—the body's energy molecule, **ATP (adenosine triphosphate)**. ATP is found in every cell in our bodies. When this energy molecule gives up its energy, it becomes **ADP (adenosine diphosphate)**. Energy is taken from glucose or another fuel to change ADP back into ATP. If all the ATP molecules stored in a muscle gave up their energy at the same time, the muscle would simply contract and then relax in exhaustion. Muscles are able to move because ATP is constantly being broken down and then built up again.

When muscles are working, they need a steady supply of ATP. The ATP for muscle fibers can be produced in two ways. In one chemical reaction, oxygen is not needed (it is called an **anaerobic**—"no-air"—reaction). Anaerobic reactions take place in the protein filaments, near where the contraction will take place. This pathway is fast. By using it, muscles can react quickly without waiting for the lungs to bring in extra oxygen, and for the heart to send the extra oxygen through the blood vessels. But the muscles can meet their energy needs with anaerobic reactions for only about two or three minutes of intense exercise.

The anaerobic reactions are also not very efficient. The waste product **lactic acid** is produced as a by-product. If a muscle works too long without much rest, a great deal of lactic acid will build up. When this happens the muscle becomes fatigued.

Too much lactic acid can poison the muscle cells. Normally, the lactic acid is carried in the bloodstream to the liver, where it may be turned back into glucose and stored away as a future source of energy. But during vigorous exercise, there isn't time to break down the lactic acid. That's why runners pant after a race, perhaps breathing even harder than they did while they were running. The body has accumulated an "oxygen debt" and needs extra oxygen to break down all of the lactic acid that has built up. So anaerobic energy reactions are used mainly when short bursts of energy are needed, as in weightlifting or sprinting. Being able to build up and then pay off an oxygen debt allows muscle cells to go on working without oxygen much longer than other body tissue—such as brain cells, which quickly die without a steady supply of oxygen.

*In contrast to anaerobic exercise, working with arm weights is a moderate form of aerobic exercise. It requires a steady oxygen supply to the muscles and can be performed over a long period of time.*

The second series of chemical reactions that muscle cells use to obtain energy is more complicated. It is an **aerobic** ("with-air") reaction pathway, which requires oxygen and uses the products that the first part of the cycle produces. It is much more efficient, producing only water, carbon dioxide, and heat as waste products. During moderate exercise—for example, jogging a couple of miles—the anaerobic pathways quickly shut down, and energy is produced aerobically. Most muscle activity uses this second part of the cycle.

The aerobic reactions take place inside small sausage-shaped cell structures called **mitochondria**. These tiny sacs of enzymes and other body substances are found all around the cell. Either glucose or fatty acids are used to build ATP. When muscles are resting, two-thirds of the aerobic energy comes from fatty acids and only one-third from glucose. Aerobic reactions supply the energy needs when muscles are at rest.

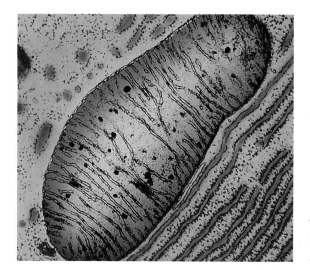

*Mitochondria are the "powerhouses" of cell activity.*

The myosin heads in muscle fibers are able to release the energy stored in ATP molecules. If muscles were 100 percent efficient, they would be able to use all of the energy from ATP for contracting. But, just as in an automobile engine, much of the energy is not converted into useful work. Instead, it is given off as heat. The heat generated by muscle contraction is a by-product that the body uses to help keep its temperature at about 98.6° F (37° C).

Excess heat is carried away from the muscles and is removed when sweat evaporates from the skin. That's why we feel hot and sweaty after vigorous exercise—there is a lot of extra heat to get rid of. When you are very cold, you may start to shiver. When you shiver, your muscles contract very rapidly and produce a great deal of heat to warm you up. Cats, dogs, and various other animals use this method to keep warm in cold weather.

*Sweating is a way for the body to get rid of excess heat.*

# HOW MUSCLE CONTRACTION IS STIMULATED

How do muscle cells know when to contract? Chemical and electrical changes cause the cell to become excited. The membrane around each cell has an electrical charge, due to the presence of charged particles called **ions**. Normally, positively charged ions, such as sodium ions, accumulate just outside a cell membrane. Like a magnet, this concentration of positively charged ions outside the cell causes negative ions to line up just inside the cell membrane.

Nerves or hormones can stimulate muscle cells. The tiny buttonlike motor end plates fit into a groove in the top of a muscle fiber, but they are not actually in contact. There is a small gap between the muscle and nerve cells. When a message is sent along the nerve to the muscle, 50 to 100 tiny sacs in the nerve ending burst open, spilling a chemical called **acetylcholine** into the space between the nerve and the muscle fiber. This messenger chemical comes in contact with the membrane of the muscle fiber. Within a few thousandths of a second, a chemical starts to break down acetylcholine. But this brief contact sets off chemical and electrical reactions that cause the muscle to contract.

Sodium cannot pass in easily through the cell membrane, and a sodium pump works to pump it out of the cell. Acetylcholine causes the membrane to allow sodium ions to rush into the muscle fiber from the fluid around the cell. This changes the electrical charge of the cell. Suddenly there is an excess of positive charges inside the cell, and an excess of negative charges outside. Almost immediately, sodium ions are pumped out of the cell, which returns to its normal state.

The change in electrical charge lasts for only 0.005 to 0.010 second, but it quickly spreads to the whole surface of the cell. A tiny current of electricity flows through the cell. This causes calcium ions stored in the cell to

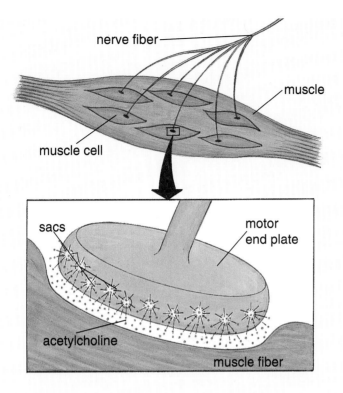

*Acetylcholine acts as a chemical messenger between*
*a motor end plate and a muscle fiber.*

be released for a few thousandths of a second, before they are absorbed once again.

Calcium ions attach to the actin filaments and remove the protective coverings, freeing active sites. So the calcium ions help make the "walk-along" mechanism work, permitting the actin filaments to slide in along the myosin filaments. Meanwhile, ATP molecules attach to the cross-bridges of the myosin filaments. Then ATP is split into ADP. The energy that is released breaks the cross-bridge links. If there were no ATP, then the actin and myosin filaments would be locked together, and the muscle fiber would be unable to move. This is actually what happens shortly after an animal dies. The muscles become stiff and locked into place, because dead cells cannot produce new supplies of ATP. The rigid state of muscle contraction that results is called **rigor mortis**.

## CONTROLLING SMOOTH MUSCLE CONTRACTIONS

The chemical reactions that take place when smooth muscle cells contract are similar to those of skeletal muscle contractions, and actin and myosin slide over one another to shorten the fiber. But some of the chemicals that cause smooth muscles in one organ to contract can cause smooth muscles in a different organ to relax. The contractions also occur much more slowly than do those in skeletal muscles.

Skeletal muscles will not contract unless they are stimulated by nerve impulses. But smooth muscle contractions can be prompted by other stimuli. Stretching of smooth muscle fibers, as in the walls of the bladder when it becomes full of urine, can trigger contractions. Hormones can also stimulate contractions.

The strength and speed of smooth muscle contractions can be changed by messages delivered by nerves. When we're nervous or afraid, for example, the intestines contract more slowly, and may even stop contracting. That's why people under a lot of stress may have trouble digesting food.

## CONTROLLING CARDIAC MUSCLE CONTRACTIONS

The contractions of the heart are begun by special cells within the heart itself. But the heartbeat rate may also be influenced by nerve impulses, hormones, and various other things.

In certain abnormal situations the heartbeat rhythm may be disturbed, and the heart may begin to contract at a very high rate (hundreds of times a minute). The individual muscle fibers lose their coordinated action; so instead of pumping, the heart muscle just quivers. This condition is called **fibrillation**. It can be a major medical emergency. Hand pumping the heart by powerful thrusts on the chest wall or applying an electric current with a special medical device can cause the heart muscle fibers to pause and then begin beating together once again.

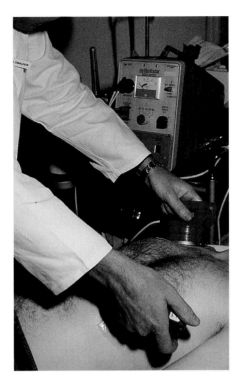

*A defibrillator is a device that uses an electric current to restore a normal heartbeat.*

# SECTION 3

Muscles of the Head and Neck

Muscles for Eating

Muscles of the Trunk

Muscles of the Arms and Hands

Muscles of the Legs and Feet

Smooth Muscles

Cardiac Muscle

Disorders of the Muscular System

Muscle Diseases

Exercise and Muscles

Rehabilitating Muscles

# MUSCLES OF THE HEAD AND NECK

In our culture everyone knows that a nod means "yes," and shaking the head means "no." A smile, a frown, a furrowed brow, a raised eyebrow, a wink, and the flaring nostrils of anger are all expressions that we may make, often unconsciously, to help express what we are feeling. Since we are able to make so many different facial expressions, it is not surprising that dozens of muscles are concentrated in this small section of the body.

In general, the muscles of the head are very thin and are attached to the skin. Beneath the skin of the scalp, for example, a single tough, muscular membrane covers the skull from the back of the head to the front just over the eyebrows. When you raise your eyebrows to indicate surprise, you are contracting the front part of this muscle.

A baby's first smile is a thrill for its parents. But even before the baby has begun to smile in response to people, it has been working on little practice smiles, frowns, and lip movements. Slowly it gains control of the many muscles that help to make the mouth area the most movable and expressive part of the face.

The most obvious muscle in the mouth area is a thick, circular (sphincter) muscle that makes up much of the lips. Other muscles in our cheeks, chin, forehead, and neck help us to make facial expressions. These muscles also help the mouth form the shapes we need to speak and to make the exact sounds we want. Usually we don't have to think about the process at all, thanks to years of practice.

Did you know that your eyes move constantly? Your lids blink once every two to ten seconds, and your eyeballs are continually jerking from one position to another. These movements are barely noticeable, but they keep the pattern of light on the retina inside the eye constantly changing. If it were possible to clamp your eyeballs in place, the sensory cells in the retina would quickly grow tired from receiving the same message over and over. Six muscles attached to each eyeball help it to move. Another muscle contracts to raise each upper eyelid. Like the bones of the skeleton, many of the muscles of the head and neck—and those of the rest of the body as well—occur in pairs, one on each side.

Above each ear are three small muscles. Most other mammals use these muscles to raise and turn their ears. Some people can use them to wiggle their ears, but in most people they don't do anything at all.

The neck is the connecting link between the head and the body. Its muscles must support the head steadily and move it when necessary. There

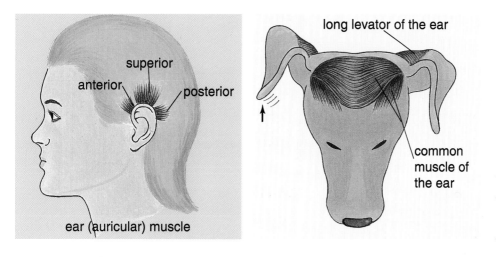

*The muscles that move a human ear (left) are much smaller than those that move a dog's ear (right).*

are also many muscles that take care of the needs of the structures in the neck. All the major supply lines of the body pass through the neck: the spinal cord (the body's main communication and control line), major air and food pipes, and important arteries and veins.

Muscles in the neck also help play an important role in forming facial expressions. You can feel the muscles in your neck when you make a wide smile or grimace. Neck muscles also help the trunk to move. They can raise the ribs to help when we breathe, help the spine move, and help in movements such as shrugging our shoulders.

The voice box, or larynx, is a muscular structure in the throat that helps us to speak. Air from the lungs flows through the voice box over two vocal cords. When the muscles in the vocal cords contract, the passing air causes them to vibrate, which produces sound, like a plucked guitar string.

# MUSCLES FOR EATING

We must eat food in order to get the nutrients that we need to keep us alive. Muscles have an important role in biting, chewing, and swallowing—the first stage in processing the foods we eat into nutrients our bodies can use.

Only the lower jaw moves when you bite and chew. The lower jaw is closed by large flat muscles that are attached from the lower jaw to the temples. These muscles are very strong, and your teeth can crush with tremendous pressure. The jaw muscles can exert a force of 200 pounds (91 kilograms)! You can feel some of the muscles that control your jaw. Clench your teeth tightly and feel for a lump above the angle of the jaw, as well as another jaw muscle contracting by your temples.

Your jaw muscles allow you to move your lower jaw in three different directions: up and down, front to back, and side to side. Moving the jaw up and down allows you to bite off chunks of food with your front teeth. The other motions help in chewing the food and grinding it to a pulp before you swallow it. Chewing your food thor-

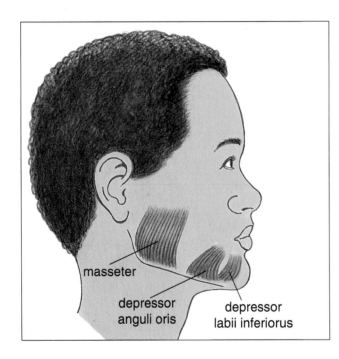

*The jaw muscles*

oughly makes it easier to digest, so that your body can get more nutrients from it. Chewing well also helps prevent large pieces of food from getting caught in your throat, which would cause you to choke.

While you chew, muscles in your lips and cheeks keep the food in the best place for the teeth to do their job. The tongue helps, too. It is mostly muscle. When the food is all ground up and mixed with saliva in your mouth, your tongue rolls it into a ball. The tongue, working with the muscles in the roof and floor of the mouth, then pushes the ball of food to the back of the mouth where it can be swallowed down into the throat.

The muscles of the palate play an important role in swallowing. They help to make sure that fluids and solids go "down the right pipe" and not into our breathing passages. If you have ever looked at your throat in a mirror, you have probably noticed a fingerlike projection dangling downward from the palate in front of the opening to the throat. This is the uvula, which contains muscles. During swallowing, these muscles raise the soft palate and act as a trapdoor, blocking off the breathing passages.

The muscles in the pharynx begin the act of swallowing. Starting to swallow is a voluntary action. But once you start, smooth muscles in the lower end of the pharynx and the esophagus take over. So once you start to swallow, you cannot stop. When you are ready to swallow, the windpipe closes and the esophagus opens up, allowing the ball of food to pass through.

## THE VERSATILE TONGUE

The tongue plays a very important role in speaking. Hold your tongue down with a finger and try to say something. If you had no tongue, people would not be able to understand anything you say. Can you roll your tongue? The ability to use tongue muscles to roll the tongue is inherited.

# MUSCLES OF THE TRUNK

You may think that the muscles in your arms are responsible for lifting a barbell over your head. But many muscles in your chest, back, and abdomen must exert a lot of energy for this task, too. Muscles in the chest and back play important roles in movements at the shoulder joints. Back muscles are involved in raising and shrugging the shoulders, extending the head and turning it from side to side, and keeping the shoulders stable when we move our arms.

The most familiar muscles in the chest are the **pectoral muscles**. Weightlifters have very strong pectoral muscles. In women, breasts are attached to these muscles. The pectoral muscles and other chest muscles help us to move our arms. Other chest muscles also help to move our arms and shoulders and help in breathing.

The many joints that make up the spine allow us to make many different movements. But this flexibility would not be possible without a complex system of muscles linking the vertebrae together. With this well-coordinated bone-muscle system, people not only can stand upright, but can also bend down and touch their toes, lift their heads to gaze up at the sky, and perform complex dances and acrobatics.

We hardly ever notice the rise and fall of the chest while we breathe, except during special circumstances—when we're trying to catch our breath after a race, for example. Spread your hands over your rib cage. Feel the walls of your chest cavity expanding upward and outward when you breathe in, and then contracting downward and inward when you breathe out. In a picture of a skeleton, the rib cage looks like a barrel-shaped cage with empty gaps between the ribs. But on a person, these gaps are filled with muscles. The chest wall is thus a solid wall, but it is not rigid—it can expand and contract, like an accordion, to help us breathe.

Most of the work in breathing is performed by the diaphragm. The sheetlike diaphragm is curved upward like a dome. When it contracts, it straightens out, moving downward. The **diaphragm** is the floor of the chest cavity and the roof of the abdominal cavity. The heart lies just above the diaphragm, and the liver and stomach fit snugly under this muscular divider. Have you ever eaten so much that you found it hard to breathe afterward? The reason was that your enlarged stomach was pressing up on the diaphragm, preventing it from contracting fully. Many muscles help us to breathe, but if necessary, the diaphragm could carry on the entire process of breathing without the help of any of the others.

The abdomen is packed with important organs. Unlike the chest and head, it has no bony cage to protect it. But the muscles of the abdominal wall provide a surprising amount of protection. See how firm the abdominal muscles get when you tense your "stomach" muscles. The structure of the abdominal muscles is a lot like a sheet of plywood. There are three muscle layers running at different angles, arranged over one another like the layers of wood placed together to form plywood.

A **hernia** can occur when gaps or spaces in the abdominal wall break open. A loop of the intestines can stick out. Usually a hernia develops after straining, for example, while lifting a heavy object or even during a very difficult bowel movement. A child can be born with a hernia, which may require surgery.

Have you ever seen the bottom fall out of a bag full of groceries? The human body would be in constant danger of dropping the abdominal organs, if it were not for the strong muscular floor that supports them.

The anal sphincter is a ring of muscle around the opening of the rectum that provides voluntary control over defecation. Babies need diapers because control over this sphincter muscle takes time to learn. This muscle is joined with an internal anal sphincter muscle that is not under voluntary control.

## A TRAGIC MISCALCULATION

The great Harry Houdini, who was famous for his ability to escape from impossible situations, used to show off his powerful abdominal muscles by having someone from the audience punch him in the belly. But one fan punched Houdini too quickly, before he had time to tense his muscles. The massive damage to his internal organs led to his death.

# MUSCLES OF THE ARMS AND HANDS

One of the most striking differences between a person and an ape is the length of the arms and legs. The arms of a gorilla or chimpanzee are far longer and stronger than those of a human being. Apes use their arms for locomotion. They swing through the trees from branch to branch. Although apes can walk upright, they usually stoop over into a four-limbed walk, partly supporting their weight on their knuckles. Humans do not use their upper limbs for locomotion. They use their arms mainly for carrying loads and for manipulating things.

*The strong arms of an orangutan are used to swing through the trees. Humans do not use their arms for locomotion.*

The arms of a rag doll hang limply at its sides. The movements of the arms of a human being would be just as limp and useless if it were not for a number of powerful muscles that connect the upper limbs to the trunk and help in movements at the shoulders.

The arms hang from the shoulders, held in place by muscles and tendons. This allows much more flexibility in movement than if they were fastened by bones. You would be unable to shrug your shoulders or raise your hand, for example, if the bones were joined together.

Muscles in the chest and back play an important role in movements of your arms at the shoulder joints. But muscles in the upper arm are also involved in these movements. If you had to spend the next few hours with your arms tied to your sides, you would find various muscles of your arms constantly tensing, even though the arms themselves could not move.

The rounded bulge on the outer surface of the upper arms is formed by the deltoid muscles. These powerful muscles cover the shoulder joint like a shield. They help us flex, extend, and rotate the arm. Injections may be given in the deltoid muscles. Other shoulder muscles help keep the shoulder joint in place.

Some of the muscles of the upper arm are involved in movements of the arm at the elbow. One of these muscles, the biceps brachii, is involved in flexing the arm. It forms a large portion of the flesh of the upper arm. The biceps works with the triceps brachii. You can feel it contracting on the back of your arm when you extend your arm.

The human hand can split a block of wood with a karate chop, thread a needle, write with a pen or a typewriter, play a musical instrument, and engage in numerous other activities that require very different movements and forces. Many muscles control the movements of the hands and fingers. Twenty pairs of these muscles are found in the forearm. Grasp the middle of your right forearm with your left hand and clench your right fist. Then stretch your fingers; then wiggle them. With each movement, you will feel muscles contracting in your forearm. You can see movement under the skin in the wrist area. But these are not muscles; they are tendons. Long tendons attach the muscles in the forearms to the hand bones. They pass under a large tendon that wraps around the wrist like a wristband.

The thumb, index finger, and little finger each have an individual mus-

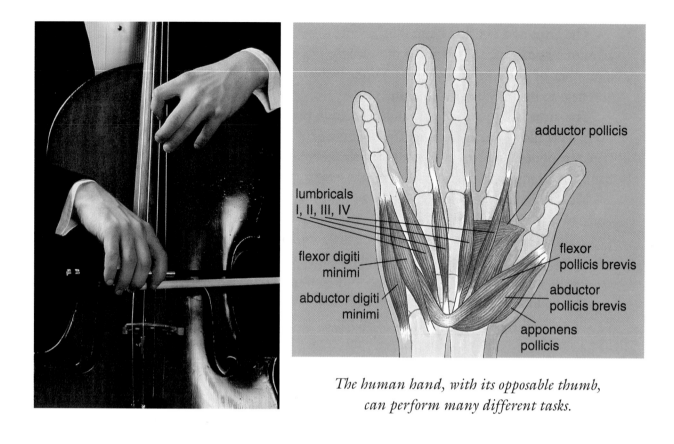

*The human hand, with its opposable thumb, can perform many different tasks.*

cle that controls extending the fingers, but the middle and ring fingers do not have a separate muscle for this action. Try moving your fingers separately. It is much easier to move those with their own extensor muscles.

About 20 small muscles in the hand help move the palm and fingers. Our hands contain many different kinds of joints, so that the muscles can move our bones in many different motions.

The hands of many animals seem similar to human hands. A squirrel sits up to eat a nut or berry, gripping its food in its "fingers" much as a person would hold a sandwich. Yet a squirrel's "hands" are not able to do as much as ours can. When a squirrel wants to pick up and carry something, it has to hold the object in its mouth—it needs its paws to walk. The major difference between human and animal hands is that we have opposable thumbs. You can easily touch the tip of your thumb to the tips of each of your fingers on the same hand. To see how limited other animals are, try touching the tip of your index finger to the tips of the other fingers.

*A squirrel can hold its food to eat, but it could never*
*develop the dexterity to play a musical instrument.*

# MUSCLES OF THE LEGS AND FEET

A typical "couch potato," watching TV while lounging on the sofa, is not making much use of his or her lower limbs. Normally, their main functions are support and movement.

In a sitting position, the weight of the body falls on the bones in the buttocks: the ischial tuberosities. The skin covering these hard bones would quickly become sore and bruised when you sat down if you did not have some good padding. Fortunately, the buttocks contain the largest mass of muscle in the body—the three **gluteal muscles**. They are also padded with fat. The muscles of the buttocks do much more than just act as a seat cushion, though. These muscles are important for moving the legs and supporting the trunk.

The muscles of the legs are similar to those of the arms, but they are a sort of heavy-duty version, designed for stability and support. They are generally stronger and heavier than arm muscles. In many cases, they allow less movement of the joints—trading flexibility for more support.

The muscles of the upper extremities usually work to move the hands from place to place. But most of the leg muscles work to move the whole body relative to the ground. Even when you are standing still, groups of leg muscles are contracting to prevent you from falling over. (Leg muscles can also work the way arm muscles do—for example, when you lie on your back and do leg-lift exercises.)

Ham and leg of lamb are cuts of meat from the thigh muscles of pigs and lambs. The human thigh is also a heavily muscled area, and its many muscles play an important role in supporting and moving the body. One thigh muscle, the ribbonlike **sartorius muscle**, is the longest muscle in the body. Its name comes from a Latin word for "tailor" because this muscle is used when we sit in the cross-legged position that old-time tailors used. The thigh, like the upper arm, has a biceps, the **biceps femoris**. The biceps and other thigh muscles in the back of our leg are sometimes called **hamstring muscles** because of their cordlike tendons, which can be felt at the back of the knee.

The **calf muscles** are among the strongest muscles of the body. When you leap and jump, a tremendous amount of force presses against your lower legs. These shocks are absorbed mainly by the calf muscles, which can withstand a force of more than a ton. The calf muscles are attached to the heel bone by the thickest and most powerful tendon in the body, the Achilles tendon. The calf muscles contract to lift the heel when you stand on your toes. The calf muscle and other muscles of the lower leg help to steady the legs in a standing position and control the movement of the feet during walking, running, and other forms of locomotion.

There are four layers of muscles in the foot, which are similar to those of the hand. But foot muscles are adapted to help the bones of the feet bear our weight and to help us move.

The big toe is provided with its own muscles for three different types of movement: moving from side to side, moving forward, and bending. The middle three toes share muscles for these types of movements. The little toe has its own muscle for moving from side to side. If you practice, you may be able to move your little toe from side to side without moving the others, but you won't be able to do it with the middle three toes.

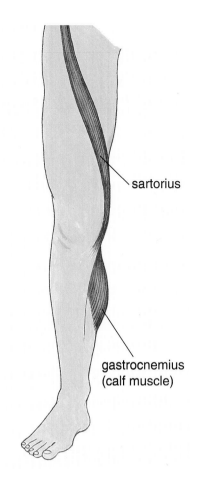

sartorius

gastrocnemius (calf muscle)

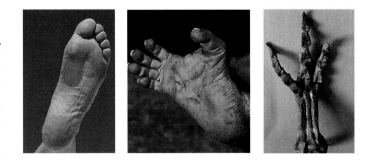

*A human foot (left) is designed for walking. A chimpanzee foot (center) is almost like a hand. The bones of a dinosaur foot (right) formed a triangle to support weight.*

# SMOOTH MUSCLES

Skeletal muscles are usually separate structures in the body, but smooth muscle is usually found inside other structures. Smooth muscles are found in the walls of many organs, such as the blood vessels, esophagus, stomach, intestines, spleen, gallbladder, and urinary bladder. Contractions of smooth muscles in the walls of the uterus push a baby on its one-way trip out into the world. Smooth muscle is found inside our eyeballs, helping to dilate our pupils. Tiny smooth muscles pull on the hair shafts in our skin. This makes the hairs stand up stiff, causing goose bumps.

If the skeletal muscle is like the hare in Aesop's fable, the smooth muscle is more like the tortoise—slow and steady. It cannot offer the huge surges of power that skeletal muscles can, but smooth muscle can go on contracting steadily day after day, without the need for frequent rests. Many processes involving movement inside the body go on all the time. Blood is always being pumped through the blood vessels, urine is constantly trickling down from the kidneys through the ureters to the bladder, and food in various stages of digestion is being pushed along the digestive tract. If the arteries, ureters, and intestines were lined with skeletal muscles instead of smooth muscles, they would quickly become tired. But the smooth muscles in these organs continue their rhythmic contractions.

Smooth muscles help to adjust the size of the

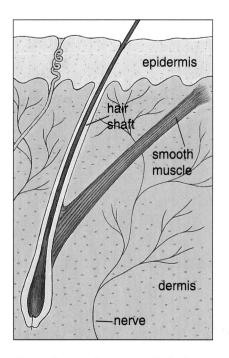

*Smooth muscles cause the hair on our skin to stand up, often in response to fear or cold. This is a reflex we share with a number of other animals.*

openings of blood vessels, and thus regulate the amount and speed of the blood flowing through them. They also help to regulate the blood pressure, providing resistance to the blood flow.

Food is pushed along the digestive system by a series of wavelike contractions. This kind of movement is called **peristalsis**. As a lump of food passes through the esophagus and intestine, circular muscles in the walls contract behind it. This squeezes the food along. Another muscle ring contracts farther down the digestive tract, pushing the food farther along. After the food has passed by, other muscles that run lengthwise in the walls of the digestive tube contract to open up the passageway again. Powerful muscles in the stomach help mix up and crush food to be digested.

Like skeletal muscles, some smooth muscles work in pairs. For example, each of your eyes has two sets of smooth muscles that control the size of your pupils. Look closely at the eyes of a friend. In the center of each eye there is a black dot. This is the pupil, an opening through which light passes into the eye. Shine the beam of a small flashlight into one eye. The pupil of that eye will quickly contract, until it is nearly as small as a pinpoint. The pupil of the other eye contracts, too. Now turn off the flashlight beam. The tiny pupil rapidly dilates, growing larger, until it is the same size it was before. The smooth muscles that cause the pupils of the eyes to contract are shaped like a ring or circle, and they are called **circular muscles**. The smooth muscles that dilate the pupils fan out like the spokes of a wheel or the radii of a circle. They are called **radial muscles**. Circular muscles contract the pupil of the eye. Radial muscles cause it to dilate.

*Smooth muscles change the size of the pupil.*

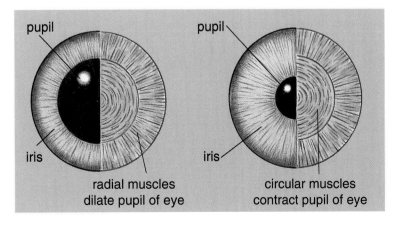

# CARDIAC MUSCLE

Your heart has been beating since about eight months before you were born, when you were only about half an inch (1.3 centimeters) long from head to toe! It has gone on beating steadily since then, with never a vacation. The cardiac muscle that makes up the walls of the heart is also called the **myocardium**. (*Cardiac* and *-cardium* both come from a word meaning "heart.") The strong contractions of this muscle produce the heartbeat.

The heart is a four-chambered organ that looks something like two ice-cream cones joined together. Blood enters the two upper chambers, called **atria**. About once every second, the thick-walled lower chambers, the **ventricles**, contract to send the blood rushing out through arteries. Blood is sent around the body to bring oxygen and nutrients to the body cells. The

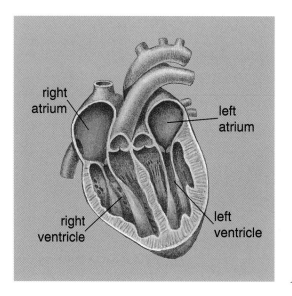

*A cross section of the heart*

heart contracts more often when you are active and your body needs more nutrients.

Most muscles can work only for a short time before they become fatigued. But cardiac muscle never gets tired. If it did, your heart would stop, and you would die. How does it keep going without resting? Actually, it doesn't. After each contraction, the heart muscle rests until the next contraction. So cardiac muscle really rests more than half the time.

In addition to muscle fibers, the heart also contains specialized cells that make up the heart's "pacemaker." This is the **sinoatrial node**, or **S-A** node. The S-A node is a natural timekeeper, which stimulates the contraction of cardiac muscle cells. It helps the heart muscle cells to contract all together, at the right pace or rhythm. Each contraction of the heart is started up by the S-A node. It sends signals to neighboring cells, causing them to contract. They prompt their neighbors to contract, and so on, so that the whole cardiac muscle works together to pump blood through the heart.

Though it normally works along steadily, cardiac muscle is capable of "shifting into high gear" for brief periods when extra stress calls for an increased supply of oxygen and nutrients—when you run to catch your bus, for example, or dash up a flight of stairs.

*Regular exercise helps to build strong heart muscle.*

# DISORDERS OF THE MUSCULAR SYSTEM

Our muscles perform amazingly well, coordinating with many different body systems. But sometimes things go wrong. For example, when skeletal muscles are used regularly and must perform vigorous contractions, the muscles grow larger and stronger. But skeletal muscles can get very sore when we exercise too hard. Muscle and connective tissue become damaged. This soreness can last for days.

The most common muscular system disorder is a **spasm**—a sudden, involuntary muscle contraction. Backaches in the lower back can be caused by muscle spasms. When a spasm continues it is called a **cramp**. If a person exercises too hard or for too long, cramps may develop. The muscle feels knotted, tense, and painful. Cramps can occur when too much lactic acid builds up. Remember, lactic acid is one of the chemicals produced when muscles contract.

Rest usually helps to stop the pain of cramps in skeletal muscles. Spasms and cramps can also occur in smooth muscles, such as the intestines or stomach. Heat, massage, or medications may be prescribed for cramps.

Muscle **strains,** or pulled muscles, occur when muscles or tendons become slightly torn. The damage may be very small, but it can cause muscle fibers to have painful spasms. Strains are usually the result of too much tension placed on the muscles.

A **sprain** is damage to a ligament (which connects bones or helps keep a joint working properly). Sprains usually happen when the area is hit in a collision or when you don't step properly.

Too much activity can damage muscles, but so can too little activity. Muscles tend to waste away when they aren't used. When muscle fibers do not contract, the actin and myosin filaments grow smaller and decrease in number. After a long period of bed rest, for example, the muscle fibers become shorter in their resting state. The muscle fibers must be exercised to bring them back to their proper length. This may be painful at first. A physical therapist may have to help move a leg into different positions, for example, if the person is not able to do it on his or her own.

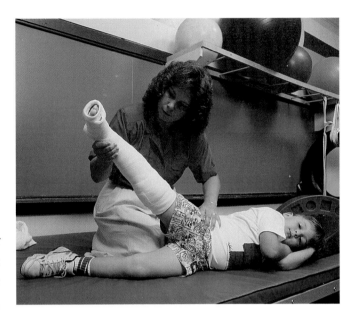

*A physical therapist works with a young person with a broken leg in order to keep the leg muscles strong.*

Muscle pain is called **myalgia**. The term **myositis** refers to an inflammation of muscular tissue. **Fibrositis** is an inflammation of the connective tissue in a muscle, usually near a joint. Sometimes people suffer from a combination of the two, fibromyositis, which is commonly called **rheumatism**.

When skeletal muscles are damaged—in an accident, for example—new muscle fibers can be formed. If there is too much damage, though, muscle tissue is replaced by scar tissue. Damaged smooth muscle and cardiac muscle cannot regrow. Scar tissue replaces it. When an artery that supplies oxygen and nutrients to the heart becomes blocked, the area of heart muscle that the artery supplies dies, and scar tissue replaces it. The scar tissue does not contract. The heart may become enlarged as it tries to make up for the damaged muscle that no longer functions. The increased contractions can be painful. If there is too much scar tissue, the heart may not be able to pump blood effectively enough to supply the body's needs.

# MUSCLE DISEASES

Pain or weakness in muscles may be the result of a simple muscle strain that just needs time to heal. But more serious health problems can also affect the muscles. Doctors today have a number of high-tech tools for diagnosing muscle diseases and disorders.

**Electromyography** (**EMG**) can be used to test how well muscles are functioning. Electrodes are placed on the skin or in the muscle to measure electrical activity. A working muscle produces tiny amounts of electricity, which form regular patterns. Abnormal readings could indicate problems. (The electrodes only pick up electricity produced by the body—they don't deliver any electricity to the patient.)

A **biopsy** (removing a small sample of tissue, which can then be examined under a microscope) is often the best way to help doctors diagnose many muscle diseases and other muscle problems. Damage to muscles can sometimes be observed with an **MRI scanner**. MRI stands for "magnetic resonance imaging." Harmless radio waves are beamed into the body and make some of the atoms in the tissues act like tiny spinning magnets. They give off characteristic signals that the MRI instrument picks up. A computer transforms the signals into a vivid picture of the internal body tissues.

Many diseases can affect the muscular system. **Myopathy** is the general category of diseases of the muscles. There are two main types of muscle diseases: those that affect the nerves that stimulate muscles and those that affect the muscles directly.

In a disease called **multiple sclerosis** the coverings of nerves in the brain or spinal column become hardened. **Lou Gehrig's disease** (also called ALS for amyotrophic lateral sclerosis) causes motor nerves in the spine and brain to slowly disintegrate. **Poliomyelitis**, or polio, is a disease caused by a virus that destroys nerve cells in the spine. In these diseases, nerves are damaged and they cannot send messages properly to the muscles. The muscles become weaker and smaller as the nerve damage becomes worse. This wasting away of the muscles is called **atrophy**. Eventually the person may become **paralyzed**, which means he or she can no longer move certain muscles voluntarily.

A person can also become paralyzed on one side of the body after suffering a stroke. In this case a part of the brain controlling body movements no longer functions properly. A stroke may occur if the blood supply is cut off to a part of the brain—when a blood vessel becomes blocked, for example.

**Muscular dystrophy** is the name for several types of inherited muscular diseases that cause the skeletal muscles to slowly waste away. Ironically, it often appears that the muscles are enlarged. But the enlargement is due to fat deposits. The actual muscle fibers waste away.

**Tetanus** is caused by a bacterium that can get into the body from a puncture wound, such as from stepping on a rusty nail. The bacteria produce a poison that blocks the normal mechanism in the body for stopping muscle contractions. The muscles become locked and immovable. Although this paralyzing disease can be fatal, it can be prevented by immunization.

In **myasthenia gravis**, abnormal antibodies are produced that prevent acetylcholine from doing its job in transmitting messages from the nerves to the muscle fibers. Eventually its victims, who are usually women, may not be able to talk, walk, swallow food, or even breathe. Some South American Indians dipped their arrows in a poison called **curare**, made from trees. This poison also works by preventing acetylcholine from doing its job, and can kill when it slows down the muscles involved in breathing.

**Botulism** is caused by a poison produced by a bacterium. Even a tiny amount prevents the release of acetylcholine at the neuromuscular junction, causing paralysis and an inability to swallow or breathe. Poisonous snakes and black widow spiders also paralyze their victims with venoms that affect the neuromuscular junction. Nerve gases used by the Nazis in World War II caused large amounts of acetylcholine to build up in the neuromuscular junction. This makes all of the muscles in the body contract, eventually preventing breathing. Some pesticides can also have the same effect.

Injury and disease can cause muscles to atrophy, but so does aging. Usually, after the age of thirty, the number and size of muscle fibers begins to decrease. Muscles become more rigid and react more slowly because connective tissue replaces some of the muscle fibers. However, regular exercise helps maintain muscle strength.

# EXERCISE AND MUSCLES

For nearly 3,000 years, physicians have recommended exercise to keep the body fit. Doctors in ancient India prescribed exercise for rheumatism. The famous Greek physician Hippocrates prescribed exercise for mental disorders. By the time of the Renaissance, a number of schools required daily exercise in addition to studies. Sports have also been important in many societies for thousands of years. Training and developing muscles and body fitness have always been an important part of preparing for competition in sports events.

*Bicycling is an aerobic exercise that increases our intake of oxygen and helps the heart and lungs grow stronger.*

Our muscles work better the more we use them, as long as we don't overdo it. Exercise helps to keep the body in shape, ready for hard work and play.

Some types of exercise help the heart and lungs to work better. When people engage in exercises such as jogging, bicycling, or swimming, they have to breathe harder to bring in more oxygen. These activities are called **aerobic exercises**.

How do aerobic exercises strengthen the heart and lungs? When we breathe, oxygen from the air is drawn into our lungs. There it passes into the network of tiny blood vessels that surround the microscopic air sacs inside the lungs. The heart pumps oxygen-carry-ing blood around the body. Muscles need oxygen when they work. So, when we exercise, more oxygen is needed, and the heart and lungs have to work harder. This makes them stronger, so that they don't have to work as hard to supply our everyday needs. A person's heart usually beats between 60 and 100 beats a minute, but an athlete's heart may beat only 40 times a minute. If we perform aerobic exercises regularly, we are able to do them for longer and longer periods of time, because the strengthened heart and lungs are able to supply the muscles' increased needs. The muscle fibers in the muscles that are exercised become better able to supply the energy that they themselves need, too. They have more myoglobin and mitochondria, as well as greater supplies of ATP.

Other types of exercise have a different effect on our muscles. Perhaps you know someone who has taken up weightlifting to develop big muscles. Some types of exercise, such as sprinting or weightlifting, require quick bursts of energy. These are called **anaerobic exercises**. When people lift heavy weights for a short time each day, their muscles grow larger. Muscle nuclei produce more protein filaments in the muscle fibers that are exer-cised. A well-trained weightlifter has no more muscle fibers than a scrawny weakling. But the weightlifter's muscle fibers are larger and contain more actin and myosin filaments in each one. There is also more connective tis-sue in the muscle. Exercise strengthens the bones and tendons, too.

*Weightlifting, when practiced regularly, is an activity that will increase the size of muscle fibers. Because weightlifting requires quick bursts of energy, it is an anaerobic exercise.*

Muscles cannot perform anaerobic exercises for very long periods because the heart and lungs cannot supply all the oxygen needed for the quick bursts of energy. The muscles quickly use up all their own stored energy.

Muscle enlargement is called **hypertrophy**. Women do not develop as big muscles as men, partly because muscle growth is somewhat controlled by testosterone, the male sex hormone. Steroid drugs are similar to the male sex hormone. That's why some body builders have used them. But they may cause some serious side effects, including liver damage, sterility, and abnormally aggressive behavior. Athletes have used other potentially harmful drugs, too, to try to push their muscles and their bodies beyond their normal abilities.

If muscles get larger when you exercise them, why do some people do exercise to lose weight and "get thin"? This kind of exercising works because contracting muscles use up energy. The body gets this energy from fat that is stored in various places, such as the belly and thighs. As people exercise, their flabby fat is used up and their muscles grow firmer. This helps to give them a thinner appearance.

These days people tend to ride most places instead of walking, and many adults have jobs that involve very little physical work. Children who are active usually get enough exercise. But many children—and even more adults—do not get enough exercise to keep themselves in shape.

A balanced program of regular exercise is very important for physical fitness. When you keep your muscles in good condition, you not only burn off extra fat but also help to keep the organs of your body properly supported so that they can work well. Walking, jogging, and swimming are especially good for a physical fitness program because they exercise many different sets of muscles, and they are activities that people can do all their lives.

## ARE MEN STRONGER THAN WOMEN?

There are many women who are stronger than many men, but overall, men generally have more muscle. Skeletal muscle makes up about 36 percent of the total body weight of women, while in men it is about 42 percent. In addition, men usually weigh more, so the amount of muscle is even greater.

Bending and stretching exercises are good warming-up and cooling-down exercises. Warming up before exercising can help prevent strains or other damage to muscle tissue. Warm-up exercises raise the temperature inside the muscles, which helps them work better. These exercises help to bring more blood to the muscles and help enzymes work better to provide energy. Cooling down when you're done exercising helps the muscles to relax now that the hard work is over. Cooling down after a strenuous workout helps to clear lactic acid from the muscles into the bloodstream, which helps prevent stiffness and fatigue.

*Stretching exercises help the muscles warm up, preparing them for more vigorous exercise.*

## EXERCISE IN OUTER SPACE

Astronauts in space have to maintain a regular exercise program to keep their muscles strong. More exercise is needed in space because under weightless conditions, without the pull of gravity for the muscles to work against, they would tend to lose their tone and even waste away.

# REHABILITATING MUSCLES

If you are sick in bed for a long time, or can't use your arm because it is in a cast, your muscles may not be able to work properly when you are well enough to use them. The muscles will be thinner, and your muscles, joints, and bones may feel stiff.

One reason weakened muscles feel stiff is that they are not getting enough oxygen. So they cannot work properly, and at first they will not be able to work for long periods at a time. But exercise helps build up weakened muscles. Massage—rubbing the muscles—can help blood to flow better, bringing more oxygen.

A person who has broken an arm or leg may not be able to use it for months. When the cast finally comes off, the help of a physical therapist may be needed to get the muscles back into shape. The physical therapist chooses exercises that help to strengthen the muscles that have become weakened.

When a person's muscles are injured in an accident, they may repair themselves after a while. Sometimes surgery can help. But even when a muscle becomes paralyzed there may still be hope. Some muscles are positioned and attached in such a way that contractions can produce several different types of movement. When a muscle is paralyzed, a physical therapist may be able to help a person learn how to use other muscles to take over the job that the paralyzed muscle is no longer able to perform. While an injured muscle is healing, or when a person's muscles can no longer support his or her weight, a cane, walker, or wheelchair may be needed.

In sports, athletes strive to have great control over the way their bodies perform. Training to build muscles for sports and rehabilitating muscles when they are injured are part of sports medicine. Athletes in training and injured athletes may use equipment designed to strengthen specific muscles. Dancers, too, may have special training programs.

Studying how people move is called **kinesiology**. A better understanding of the way we move is useful for training in sports and dance. Using computers, trainers and instructors can analyze an athlete's or dancer's performance to find tiny flaws that need improving. A better understanding of movement also helps trainers to determine the proper exercises for people in training as well as for those with injuries.

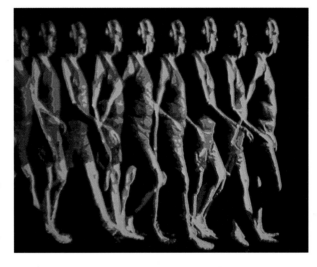

*Photographic and computerized studies of how we move are useful in sports training and in medicine.*

The study of motion and muscle movement is also helping scientists to develop artificial limbs and other devices to help people with paralyzed muscles. One advance is the EMG or electromyograph, which records electrical activity in muscles. Electrodes are placed on the skin or in the muscle. The instrument translates the electrical changes that occur when a muscle contracts into flashing lights and buzzing sounds. This provides the person with feedback for learning how to control the contraction of particular motor units. Some people can learn to make a single motor unit fire at will. EMG biofeedback has helped a number of patients with spinal cord injury and patients who have suffered strokes to strengthen their muscles—and in several cases to restore some ability to use their muscles.

For many years, researchers have been trying to use EMG signals to operate artificial limbs. As electronic parts have been made smaller and smaller, the prospects have become more promising. There have already been some successes. A metal and plastic prosthetic device called the Boston elbow contains a battery-powered motor. Electrodes attached to the skin of the forearm pick up electrical signals when the person flexes muscles in his or her arm. These signals cause the motor to open or close the artificial hand. Scientists hope that artificial limbs in the future will allow much finer movements.

Researchers are also working on prosthetic limbs that are directly controlled by nerve signals. Electrodes are implanted around motor nerves. These electrodes pick up messages sent through the nervous system and forward them to a transmitter, which then relays the messages to the artificial limb. This type of prosthetic limb would allow a greater variety of movement and more natural movements.

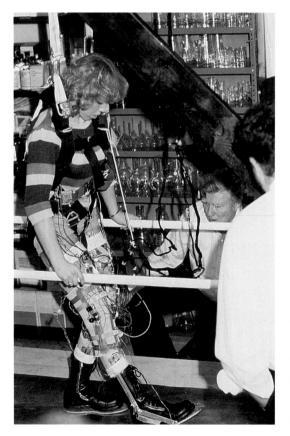

*Although paralyzed from the waist down, this patient is able to walk with the help of a computer. The computer controls muscle stimulation in the legs.*

Scientists are using tiny computers to send electrical impulses to paralyzed limbs to make them move when the person wants them to. The computer takes over for the brain to coordinate the movements of groups of muscles.

As scientists' understanding of our muscular system grows, so will the ways that medicine can help to improve our muscles' abilities. Their research will also bring new ways of helping people who are physically handicapped to lead more normal lives.

# GLOSSARY

**acetylcholine**—a neurotransmitter chemical, which aids in transmitting messages from nerve cells to muscle fibers.

**Achilles tendon**—the tendon attaching the calf muscle to the heel bone.

**actin**—one of the contractile proteins responsible for muscle action.

**ADP (adenosine diphosphate)**—the chemical form to which ATP is converted when it gives up its stored energy.

**aerobic**—occurring in the presence of air.

**aerobic exercises**—activities that stimulate breathing and circulation, bringing more air into the body and more oxygen to the body cells.

**anaerobic**—occurring in the absence of air.

**anaerobic exercises**—activities that require quick bursts of energy, such as sprinting or weightlifting.

**antagonists**—paired muscles that work against each other.

**appendicular muscles**—muscles of the arms and legs.

**ATP (adenosine triphosphate)**—a chemical used in the body to store energy.

**atrium**—the upper chamber of each side of the heart. (Plural: atria.)

**atrophy**—the wasting away of a body part or tissue.

**auxin**—a plant hormone that controls growth of plant cells.

**axial muscles**—muscles of the head, neck, and trunk.

**belly**—the rounded middle part of a skeletal muscle.

**biceps femoris**—the thigh muscle whose contractions bend the leg at the knee.

**biceps muscle**—the muscle in the upper arm that bends the arm at the elbow; the biceps brachii.

**biopsy**—removal of a small sample of tissue for microscopic examination.

**botulism**—severe food poisoning in which a bacterial toxin prevents the release of acetylcholine at the neuromuscular junction, resulting in paralysis.

**buoyancy**—the tendency of water to hold up things placed in it (if they are not denser than water).

**calf muscle**—the gastrocnemius muscle; the large muscle at the back of the lower leg.

**cardiac muscle**—heart muscle.

**circular muscles**—the ring-shaped muscles that contract the pupils of the eyes.

**contraction**—shortening; the action of a muscle that may produce movement of a body part.

**cramp**—a prolonged muscle spasm.

**cross-bridges**—temporary connections between the myosin heads and actin fibers as they slide past each other.

**curare**—a nerve poison that blocks the neurotransmitter acetylcholine, preventing the transmission of nerve impulses to muscles.

**diaphragm**—a dome-shaped sheet of muscle that forms the floor of the chest cavity.

**EMG (electromyography)**—measurement of the electrical activity of working muscles with electrodes placed on the skin or in the muscle.

**extensor**—a muscle that straightens a joint or extends a limb.

**fast-twitch fibers**—large muscle cells that contract quickly, providing for strength and power.

**fatigue**—tiredness; a weakening of a muscle that has been working, due to the buildup of chemical wastes and depletion of glucose and oxygen.

**fibrillation**—uncoordinated contraction of cardiac muscle fibers, resulting in quivering instead of pumping.

**fibrositis**—inflammation of connective tissue in a muscle, usually near a joint.

**flexor**—a muscle that brings two body parts closer together, e.g., one that bends a limb at a joint.

**fulcrum**—the pivot of a lever.

**gastrocnemius muscle**—the calf muscle in the back of the lower leg.

**glucose**—a simple sugar; the body's main energy fuel.

**gluteal muscles**—the buttocks muscles.

**glycogen**—animal starch; an energy storage chemical made up of thousands of glucose units.

**hamstring muscles**—the thigh muscles, whose cordlike tendons can be felt at the back of the knee.

**hernia**—a gap or space in the abdominal muscles, which may permit a loop of intestine to stick out.

**hypertrophy**—enlargement (e.g., of muscles).

**insertion**—the end of a skeletal muscle that is attached to a bone that moves when the muscle contracts.

**involuntary muscles**—muscles that work automatically, without conscious control.

**ion**—an electrically charged chemical particle.

**isometric contraction**—contraction (tensing) of a muscle that does not result in its shortening.

**isotonic contraction**—muscle action accompanied by shortening of the muscle.

**kinesiology**—the study of how people move.

**lactic acid**—the waste product of anaerobic reactions that supply energy in muscle cells. Buildup of lactic acid causes muscle fatigue.

**lever**—a simple machine that multiplies the force applied.

**locomotion**—movement of the whole body from one place to another.

**Lou Gehrig's disease**—amyotrophic lateral sclerosis (ALS); a disease in which motor nerves in the brain and spinal cord gradually disintegrate.

**mitochondria**—structures inside cells in which ATP is produced.

**motor end plates**—the buttonlike endings of motor nerves.

**motor nerves**—nerves that carry messages from the brain to the muscles, glands, and other body structures, resulting in actions.

**motor strips**—portions of the cerebral cortex controlling voluntary actions.

**motor unit**—a motor neuron and the muscle fibers it controls.

**MRI scanner**—device for observing damage to muscles and other tissues by magnetic resonance imaging.

**multiple sclerosis**—a disease in which the coverings of nerves in the brain or spinal column become hardened, making the transmission of nerve impulses to muscles less effective.

**muscle fiber**—a muscle cell.

**muscle spindles**—proprioceptors that report to the brain when muscle fibers stretch.

**muscle tone**—a slight contraction of a muscle due to the fact that some of the muscle cells are contracting at any particular time.

**muscular dystrophy**—one of several inherited muscular diseases in which the skeletal muscles slowly waste away.

**myalgia**—muscle pain.

**myasthenia gravis**—an autoimmune disease in which antibodies against the neurotransmitter acetylcholine block the transmission of nerve impulses to muscles.

**myocardium**—the heart muscle (cardiac muscle).

**myofibrils**—thinner fibers that make up a muscle fiber.

**myofilaments**—thin strands of muscle proteins (actin and myosin) that make up the myofibril.

**myoglobin**—a pigment (similar to hemoglobin) that makes muscle cells red.

**myopathy**—disease of the muscles.

**myosin**—one of the contractile proteins responsible for muscle action.

**myositis**—inflammation of muscular tissue.

**neuromuscular junction**—the meeting point of a motor nerve ending and a muscle fiber.

**origin**—the end of a skeletal muscle that is attached to a bone that does not move when the muscle contracts.

**paralysis**—inability to move body parts (i.e., to use voluntary muscles) and/or loss of sensation.

**pectoral muscles**—chest muscles.

**peristalsis**—wavelike contractions of smooth muscles that move the contents of tubular organs along (for example, in the digestive system).

**poliomyelitis**—polio; a viral disease that destroys nerve cells in the spine.

**proprioceptors**—sensory organs that report on the status of muscles and internal organs.

**radial muscles**—the muscles that dilate (widen) the pupils of the eyes.

**reflex actions**—automatic actions in reaction to a stimulus, performed very rapidly without conscious thought or decision.

**rheumatism**—fibromyositis; inflammation of muscle and connective tissue, usually near a joint.

**rigor mortis**—the rigid state of the body after death due to irreversible muscle contractions.

**sartorius muscle**—a long muscle in the thigh.

**sinoatrial (S-A) node**—the pacemaker; a portion of the heart muscle on the right atrium whose rhythmic contractions set the heartbeat rate.

**skeletal muscles**—muscles that work with bones of the skeleton; also called voluntary muscles.

**sliding filament theory**—the theory that muscle contraction occurs when actin and myosin filaments slide past each other until they overlap.

**slow-twitch fibers**—smaller muscle cells that contract slowly and steadily and provide for endurance.

**smooth muscles**—muscles that do not work with bones; in humans, also called involuntary muscles.

**spasm**—a sudden, involuntary muscle contraction.

**sphincter**—a circular muscle that contracts to narrow or close an opening.

**sprain**—damage to a ligament (connecting bones in a joint).

**stimulus**—a signal that prompts an action.

**strain**—a pulled muscle; injury producing a slight tear in a muscle or tendon.

**striated muscle**—skeletal muscle, named for the stripes (striations) visible under a microscope.

**tendon**—tough, whitish, cordlike tissues that attach muscles to bones.

**tetanus**—a bacterial disease in which toxins block muscle relaxation and the muscles become locked and immovable.

**turgor**—firmness. (The turgor of plant cells depends on the amount of water inside them.)

**ventricles**—the thick-walled muscular lower chambers of the heart; the pumping chambers.

**voluntary muscles**—skeletal muscles; muscles that can be controlled at will.

# TIMELINE

## B.C.

**1000**   Physicians in India recommended exercise for rheumatism.

**400**   Aristotle (Greek philosopher) described how animals move.

## A.D.

**200**   Galen (Greek physician) showed that muscles work in pairs and pull on bones, but believed "animal spirits" caused muscles to contract.

**1500**   Leonardo da Vinci (Italian artist) attached wires to a skeleton to study how muscles work and made detailed drawings.

**mid-1600s**   Francis Glisson (English physician) showed that muscles contract, rather than expand.

**1700**   Antonie van Leeuwenhoek (Dutch microscopist) saw stripes in skeletal muscles under a microscope.

**1700**   Giorgio Baglivi (Italian physician) distinguished between skeletal and smooth muscles.

**late 1700s**   Luigi Galvani (Italian scientist) discovered that electricity transmitted from nerves makes muscles contract.

**1878**   English photographer Eadweard Muybridge used motion-picture photography to observe animal movements.

**1945**   Researchers discovered osteogenin, a substance that induced rabbit muscle to become bonelike.

**1950**   American and British researchers (Hugh Huxley and Andrew Huxley) independently developed the sliding filament theory of muscle contraction.

**1988**   Researchers discovered a muscle protein (dystrophin) not found in muscular dystrophy patients.

**1991**   Researchers stimulated the formation of bone in muscle tissue.

**1992**   Patches delivering the male hormone testosterone were used to improve muscle strength of elderly men.

**1992**   Researchers found a gene leading to muscular dystrophy.

**1993**   Researchers used gene therapy to correct muscular dystrophy in mice.

# INDEX